I0027923

Jews of Nigeria

An Afro-Judaic Odyssey

ALSO BY WILLIAM F. S. MILES

My African Horse Problem

Zion in the Desert.
American Jews in Israel's Reform Kibbutzim

Political Islam in West Africa.
State-Society Relations Transformed (ed.)

Bridging Mental Boundaries in a Postcolonial Microcosm.
Identity and Development in Vanuatu

Imperial Burdens.
Countercolonialism in Former French India

Hausaland Divided.
Colonialism and Independence in Nigeria and Niger

Paradoxe au Paradis.
De la politique à la Martinique

Elections in Nigeria.
A Grassroots Perspective

Elections and Ethnicity in French Martinique

Jews of Nigeria

An Afro-Judaic Odyssey

WILLIAM F. S. MILES

Markus Wiener Publishers
Princeton

Copyright © 2013 Markus Wiener Publishers,
Princeton, New Jersey

All rights reserved. No part of this book may be reproduced
or transmitted in any form or by any means, whether electronic
or mechanical—including photocopying or recording—or through
any information storage or retrieval system, without permission
of the copyright owners.

Photographs: All photos, including the cover image,
are by William F. S. Miles.

For information, write to:
Markus Wiener Publishers
231 Nassau Street, Princeton, NJ 08542
www.markuswiener.com

Library of Congress Cataloging-in-Publication Data

Miles, William F. S.
  Jews of Nigeria : an Afro-Judaic odyssey / William F. S. Miles.
  p. cm.
  ISBN 978-1-55876-565-8 (hardcover : alk. paper)
  ISBN 978-1-55876-566-5 (pbk. : alk. paper)
  1. Jews—Nigeria. 2. Judaism—Nigeria.
  3. Igbo (African people)—Nigeria—Religion. I. Title.
  BM440.N6M55 2013
  296.09669—dc23
    2012018759

Markus Wiener Publishers books are printed in the United States
of America on acid-free paper and meet the guidelines for permanence
and durability of the Committee on Production Guidelines for
Book Longevity of the Council on Library Resources.

To My Jewish Brothers in Nigeria,
Habakkuk and Pinchas and the Rest

To Rabbi Howard Gorin,
Who First Introduced Them to Me

To Rabbi Wayne Franklin,
For His Ecumenical and Spiritual Support

and

To Rabbi Joel Seltzer,
For His "Sizzling" Responses to My African Wanderings

Contents

Judaism in Black Africa:
Ancient (Ethiopian) and Emerging (Nigerian)

A Religio-Autobiographic Prolegomenon

(Otherwise Known as "Preface and Acknowledgments")

There is always something new out of Africa.
—Pliny the Elder (A.D. 23-79), *Historia Naturalis*

Who is wise? He who learns from all people.
—Simeon ben Zoma (c. A.D. 100-133), *Pirkei Avot*

Taken together these two insights, commonly attributed to the classical-era Roman scholar Pliny and the Tannaidic (pre-Talmudic) teacher ben Zoma, convey a major message of this book: that all people, Jewish as well as not, have much to learn from Africa. The "new thing out of Africa" that this book highlights is the emerging community of Nigerians, mostly Igbos, who only in recent years have discovered (or, according to many of them, rediscovered) Judaism. The existence of this unexpected and budding Jewish community in the world's largest Black nation should be of interest to all who follow contemporary trends in Africa or are intrigued by new religious movements across the world.

But Jews in particular do have something to learn from—or to wrestle with—on account of this "new thing out of Africa": the very meaning of Jewishness and their personal identity as Jews. I know I have. (I have also learned from scholars Feinberg and Solodow [2002] that Pliny is not the original source of the "something new out of Africa" quotation.) Encountering observant Nigerian Jews in their own homes and synagogues has been a profoundly moving experience, even for this seasoned social scientist who had already been going to Africa for more than thirty years and speaks one of Nigeria's major languages. *Not* to convey the subjective dimension to these encounters would have been to artificially strip this book of an important element of that experience.

Secular (or self-styled "ethnic") Jews tend to tackle questions of Jewishness and Jewish identity differently from religious Jews; Judaism, the religious dimension, becomes the usual dividing line. But on account of complicated (and usually taboo) questions of race and ethnocentrism, the new phenomenon of Nigerian Jewry presents a challenge to both kinds of Jews. Remember, both in terms of geography and genealogy, we are far from Ethiopia. There, practitioners of an ancient form of Judaism (who previously—despite its pejorative etymology—were commonly referred to as Falashas) occupied a long and heralded chapter in Jewish history. Indeed, their chapter turned outright heroic with the Exodus-like exploit of their massive air lifts from Marxist Ethiopia to the State of Israel in the 1980s and 1990s. Today, relatively few "Falashas"— including most of their Falash Mura cousins (Christians whose ancestors had been Jewish)—are left in Ethiopia. In short, the storied history of African Jews, claiming descent from King David and the Queen of Sheba and living out an ancient Israelite existence in East Africa, is now practically a closed chapter.

Unlike Ethiopia, Nigeria, for many casual followers of the continent, conjures up very different connotations: unpleasant memories of e-mail scams and other unsavory associations. At a time when Israel is forcefully cracking down on thousands of illegal immigrants from throughout sub-Saharan Africa, the prospect of thousands of Nigerians claiming a Jewish identity typically prompts more apprehension than enthusiasm among those who identify with Judaism or with the Jewish State, or with both. Aside from the Jewish angle, as someone who has followed the country regularly since spending a State Department summer in 1980 at the American Consulate in Kaduna, I had long come to view supposedly wonderful "new things out of Nigeria" with a skeptical, if not jaded, eye. So when I initially chanced upon an article in a Jewish magazine (Palmer 2006) about the peripatetic Rabbi Howard Gorin of Maryland, dubbed by his new flock of followers in West Africa the

"Chief Rabbi of Nigeria," I mentally consigned the story to that collection of Nigerian oddities to be treated with due caution. Ditto for the works of the Yoruba Hebraicist Modupe Oduoye, whom I had the good fortune of encountering in Ibadan in 2001.[1] Intriguing and eclectic, but eccentric and fanciful. Who could take such things seriously? What scholar could? What Jew?

Imagine my stupefaction, then, when Edith Bruder's *The Black Jews of Africa* landed, as a book review assignment, on my desk. There, I read serious scholarship about multiple communities of Nigerians who, in only the last couple of decades, have come to practice Judaism. Most of them are Igbos, a southern people to whom I had had relatively little exposure. But some Igbos were establishing themselves as far north as Abuja, the capital in the center of the country, where I had recently conducted research on Islamic politics. How could I have been so near to them so recently, and yet not heard of, much less encountered, them? Thanks to Rabbi Howard Gorin and Abuja attorney and human rights activist Hauwa Ibrahim, I returned to Abuja to spend Hanukka in 2009 (Miles 2011) among those whom I have come to call "Jubos": Igbos who practice Judaism.[2] It was there and then that I first met Sar Habakkuk of Tikvat Israel, Pinchas ben Eliezer of Gihon Hebrew Research Centre, Remy Ilona the Jubo historian, and the others whom I introduce in chapter one ("First Encounters with Jubos"). Abdulmalik Badamassi, a non-Igbo on his own quest for Hebraic roots, greatly assisted me during that visit. Chapter two revolves around my return in August 2011 for the first bar mitzvah of the Tikvat Israel community in Abuja, when I met for the first time other Jubos who traveled great distances to attend the *simcha* [Hebrew: joyous celebration] for Hezekiah ben Habakkuk. In chapter three ("In Their Own Words: Jubos Describe Their Spiritual

---

[1] "[T]here is little specifically Jewish in . . . the first eleven chapters of Genesis . . . and yet a lot that is Afro-Asiatic," Oduoye, who studied theology at Yale, writes in the preface to his "Afro-Asiatic Interpretation of Genesis."

[2] I am aware that to some ears "Jubo" sounds humorous; for some it is funny even to the point of parody. Nothing could be further from my intention.

Journey"), I directly relate the life stories, as I recorded and tran-
scribed them, of resident members of Tikvat Israel and Gihon congregations in Abuja and visitors from Ogidi Jewish Community
Synagogue; the quotation that appears under each portrait photo is
my composite of compelling speaker points, whose verbatim ex-
pression appears in the text itself. In chapter four, we tour a remarkable shrine, a unique example of syncretism between
normative Judaism and indigenous African spirituality. A postscript
relates the mutual astonishment when I met with the eminent
Nigerian author Chinua Achebe and shared with him my encounters with his fellow Igbos who practice Judaism.

Listening to my field recordings, and hearing the ambient
sounds that I had cognitively suppressed in real time so as to focus
on my interlocutors, recalled for me a strange sensation of displace-
ment: at some level, Abuja felt like Jerusalem. That, I realized in
playback mode, was because our discussions of purely Jewish matters were often punctuated, in the background, by muezzins' call
to the mosque. Outside of Israel (and, to a lesser extent, Morocco),
where does this occur on a routine basis: Jewish communities
freely living out their daily lives to an Islamic soundtrack?

The recorded voices reflect the wide range in facility in the English language and, by implication, in formal education, among the
Abuja Jubos. This is only partly apparent from the interview tran-
scripts. Some members of the congregation speak a most cultivated
English, and my transcriptions of them are virtually literal; the
speech of others who have not had the benefit of long-term studies
required intensive editing for the sake of fluidity. Those Jubos ar-
ticulate in English spoke to me on tape for nearly an hour; some
of the others exhausted what they needed to say in barely five minutes. Even among the most eloquent of the Jubos, different usages
of context and vocabulary (particularly in the religious realm) require due care for understanding. To cite one example: whereas
"Orthodox Judaism" is ordinarily used to distinguish it from the
Conservative, Reform, and Reconstructionist branches of the religion, in Nigeria the term emerges foremost in contradistinction to
"Messianic" (i.e., Jesus-worshiping) Judaism—which, of course,

is not usually considered by world Jewry to be congruent with contemporary Judaism at all. For several Jubos, God is seen to guide His chosen people indirectly, pragmatically, employing preexisting pathways that will facilitate their homeward spiritual journey. In the context of Nigeria, this means using Messianic Judaism as a bridge, back from the Christianity that missionary colonialism had imposed on Igbos and towards the real Judaism that is their ancestral inheritance.

Most difficult to convey on paper is the *tone* of voice I recorded in my interviews: the earnestness, yearning, and poignancy with which Jubos describe their individual searching for the proper path to God, and the right way in which to worship Him. As they describe their first encounter with Judaism, their voices convey another revelation: Judaism is exciting! For them it is new, a wholly novel way of life, a different way of looking at the world and acting within it. For any Jew who is already the heir to hundreds if not thousands of years of Jewish culture and religion, seeing a community's initial engagement with the Hebraic tradition is almost like being jolted back to Sinai. No Jew, engaged or detached, believing or not, can be indifferent when exposed to the soulful embrace and exciting encounter with Jewishness by Torah-following West Africans.

The Jubos in Abuja constitute a Jewish community in the fullest sense, encompassing members from a broad socioeconomic spectrum. They range from petty traders, launderers, and realtors to civil servants, engineers, and a hospital surgeon. One describes himself as "spiritual healer." Most of the adult women are homemakers, and they take their responsibility for making *Jewish* homes quite seriously. Younger Jewish girls have opportunities for education, general and Jewish, that their mothers did not. It will be fascinating to see how the Jewishness of these girls affects their societal roles and ambitions as they enter adulthood.

For all their differences in region, culture, and ethnicity, Nigerians across the board do share one important national trait: they are an intensely religious people. The search for spiritual truth is a daily, existential preoccupation in Nigeria: no Western-style divi-

sion here into religious and public spheres (what in the United
States falls under the oft-abused catchphrase "separation of church
and state"). Much media reporting on Nigeria, focusing as it does
on communal violence, contributes to our confusion of religiosity
with sectarianism. But Nigerians are a religious people in that the
individual's search for correct spiritual belief and practice is as
front and center an aspect of daily life as is the struggle to secure
more naira (the local currency). It is in this sense that the Jubos are
both very Jewish and very Nigerian. By taking their newly found
(or rather, as they see it, rediscovered) Judaism as seriously as they
do, they are also reflecting the very Nigerian penchant to be outwardly and inwardly secure in their relationship with God. Emphasis on collective identity and responsibility is another
Nigerian/African cultural trait that blends into their Judaism: Dr.
Caliben's address at the bar mitzvah reception, we shall see, is directed not so much to the celebrant Hezekiah himself as it is to the
entirety of the community, to Hezekiah's age cohorts and their parents. Overall, the Jubos' most earnest goal, it must be emphasized,
is normative Judaism: to practice the "correct" way, the way it is
recognized by the Jewish world at large.

The complication, of course, is that in the twenty-first century,
the "Jewish world at large" is far from united as to what constitutes
the correct way of practicing Judaism. Newly Jewish or re-judaized
communities are potential new battlegrounds in the longstanding
legitimacy struggle between the Orthodox stream of Judaism on
the one hand and non-Orthodox (particularly Conservative and Reform) streams on the other. Undercurrents of difference between
Orthodox and non-Orthodox versions of Judaism already play out
in Nigeria around such issues as a synagogue partition between
men's and women's seating sections (yes in Gihon, no in Tikvat
Israel). And what to make of the Jubo custom of ablution: ritual
hand washing before entering the House of Worship for each discrete prayer service? Should it be viewed as the resurrection of a
once *halachic* (i.e., legally Jewish) custom or as a Jubo innovation?
How should Jews comfortable with saying the *hamotzi* prayer over
challah bread react to the comparable Jubo blessing over the kola

nut? Where did the custom of exiting the synagogue backwards, in song, at the end of Shabbat come from? (It symbolizes both reluctance for the Sabbath to end and continued orientation during the regular week toward the faith.) However endearing these practices are, some Jewish skeptics will inevitably also wonder: how can one know if the Jubos' lifelong quest for spiritual truth (some of the previous denomination-hopping described in the interviews is quite extraordinary in this regard) will have definitively ended with their embrace of normative Judaism?

Jubos themselves are quite cautious in this regard, as evidenced in the ongoing enumeration (the first ever) of the Jewish population of Nigeria. "We are being careful in our census. It is not really all people who say they are Jewish in worship who truly are. There are some Messianics who say they are. Some will say *shema*,[3] keep Shabbat, but at the end of the day pray *b'shem Yehoshua ha-Moshiach* [Hebrew: in the name of Jesus the Messiah] . . ."

In the same vein, Benson Usiade, a true Jubo working as an architect in California, is said to have met on a plane returning home another Nigerian who said he was Jewish. Benson reportedly asked, "Oh, do you have a Sefer Torah in your synagogue, in your community?"

"Yes, we do," replied the fellow passenger, "and we read it from Genesis through Revelation!"[4] Along with his interlocutors in Abuja, the teller of this story erupted into laughter, adding, in an earnest tone, "You really have to be careful."

* * *

---

[3] The *shema* [Hebrew: hear] is the quintessential prayer of Judaism: "Hear O Israel, the Lord The God, the Lord is One."

[4] The Torah scroll is a handwritten transcription on parchment of the first section of the Old Testament, otherwise known as the Five Books of Moses (Genesis, Exodus, Leviticus, Numbers, Deuteronomy). The Book of Revelations is a quintessentially New Testament work, one that no "true Jew" would acknowledge as part of Hebrew scripture.

Given the egalitarian momentum within the Jewish world at large, in the life stories readers will be taken aback at certain Jubo references to women. These include the ideal of wives following the (spiritual) decisions of their husbands and the overt preference for having male children. In this sense, too, the Jubos reflect their Igbo cultural roots, common West African attitudes, even. But this inclination too must be put into perspective, for when it comes to female respect and autonomy, Igbos are generally considered to be much more enlightened than their northern Nigerian and Muslim compatriots. Jubos are undoubtedly making West Africa more Jewish. When it comes to gender issues, however, Judaism is not (yet?) making Jubos less Igbo.

Jubos are probably the world's first Internet Jews. While much of their phenomenal mastery of Jewish practice and Hebrew prayer comes from diligent, traditional study (albeit through photocopies) of religious books and Hebrew language texts, their transition out of "Messianic" to normative Judaism happened to coincide with the computerization and global wiring of Nigeria. Google has undoubtedly accelerated and intensified the Juboization of Nigeria, as access to once arcane Judaica has come as close as the nearest cyber café. Jubos in Abuja were early adopters of Rabbi Howard Gorin's weekly commentaries on the Torah reading from his website *Shalom, Africa*. But even in a few short years, Jubos went beyond that. "Thanks to technology," one Jubo tells me, "we can now access different rabbis on line. Weekly *parshiot* [Hebrew: Torah readings] and commentaries. Today, in addition to *Shalom, Africa* we also have Chabad.org and the Hasidic masters." Still, he reminds me, "Self-learning cannot be the same as when you have a trained rabbi on ground." The absence of a resident Jewish teacher is bemoaned over and over.

Online and journalistic accounts of the Jubos occasionally appear; see, for example, Lis 2006 and Perelman 2008. But for a scholarly treatment of the Jubos beyond Abuja, we must await the completion and dissemination of Daniel Lis's doctoral dissertation; in the meantime, Lis's account (2009) of an intriguing encounter between Ethiopian and Igbo Jews in Israel is recommended. Also

in need of future tracking is Nigerian response to Jeffrey Lieberman's newly released documentary film, *Re-Emerging: The Jews
of Nigeria*. To appreciate the indigenous perspective that reflects
burgeoning West African (qua Igbo) attempts to reclaim a Hebraic/
Israelite/Jewish identity as descendants of the tribe of Gad, one
must read I.O. Michael Caliben (2011), Remy Ilona (n.d., 2007,
2012), and Charles Ujah (2006).[5] Associations like the Ibo Benei-
Yisrael Association of Nigeria and the Obgi[6] Israel Heritage Foundation, while producing their own materials, make similar ancestral
claims. Related, in terms of Jewish-African borrowings, is the collection by Yosef Ben-Jochannan et al. (1988).

I wish to stress, however, that according to my own primary research into the Judaization of contemporary Igbos, theology trumps
genealogy; that is, having first been drawn away from Christianity
towards Judaism for reasons of faith, doctrine, and logic, they have
retrospectively imputed cultural affinities between Jewish and Igbo
traditions traceable to a Hebraic ancestry. They did not *first* decide
that they were a "Lost Tribe" of Israel and consequently begin to
learn and appropriate modern Judaism; rather, only after they had
begun to embrace normative Judaism in their quest for spiritual
truth did they perceive commonalities between their indigenous
Igbo traditions and normative Jewish practice.[7] Igbo traditions re-
inforced Jubos' identification with Judaism but did not initiate it.

But are they "really" Jews? Who, after all, *is* a Jew?

The longstanding traditional answer is the one of Orthodoxy: a
Jew is one born of a Jewish mother or one who has converted

---

[5] Ujah (2006: ix) also includes other southern Nigerian tribes (Calabars,
Ibibio, Idomas, Ijaws, Isokos Ogojas, Tivs, and Urhobos) among the "Hebrew
of Nigeria."

[6] "OBGI is nothing other than IGBO in reverse writing. Why reverse writing?
Our activities, behaviours, total output leaves much to be desired. ... [T]oday
we are the exact opposite of what we used to be." From page 1 of the Obgi Israel
Heritage Foundation presentation booklet.

[7] For an interesting discussion of the "Lost Tribes" phenomenon from the anthropological perspective, see Kirsch (1997).

through the Orthodox Jewish rabbinate.[8] But without Jewish up-
bringing or education, that "Jew" may never even know he or she
is Jewish. Is he or she? Close to our own tragic times, how many
offspring of Holocaust survivors never did learn—as former secretary of state Madeleine Albright and documentary filmmaker
Pierre Sauvage did accidentally find out, after they had grown up—
that their parents had been Jewish but deemed it too dangerous to
pass on Jewish identity to their children? How many more, in less
existentially fraught times, have jettisoned Jewish religion and
identity out of inconvenience, indifference, or opportunism (Rubin
1995)?

Let's go back in time. Think of the countless millions of human
beings inhabiting the earth today who had Jewish ancestors, but
who are not themselves Jewish. Through conversion (forced or vol-
untary), intermarriage, or plain indifference, their forefathers (and,
more important, their foremothers) ceased being Jewish. The vast
majority of those non-Jewish descendants of Jews have no idea
about their Jewish ancestry. It is lost to family history. Probably,
these descendants would not even want, or care, to know. Why
should they? Many of them have long since adopted another religion and ethnicity. Their identity, as individuals and collectively,
is anything but Jewish. There is something unseemly about others
retroactively attributing to such individuals a Jewish heritage or
identity. It is obviously objectionable when anti-Semites do it. But
on principle I also find it intrusive when philo-Semites, or Jews
themselves—unasked, unbidden, uninvited—do so.

In short, I am opposed to the notion of "DNA Jewry": of im-
parting to people who themselves do not identify as Jews, sheerly
on the basis of genes or chromosomes, a putative Jewish identity,
kinship, or bond.[9]

Now what has this got to do with the Jews of Nigeria? Ortho-
praxy, I submit in this case, ought to trump orthodoxy. In other

---

[8] Reform Judaism has adoped paternal descent, as long as the parents agree
to raise the child Jewishly.
[9] Goldstein's (2008) "genetic view of Jewish history" is an example of the
kind of approach that makes me leery.

words, the fact that the individuals you will encounter in this book live as Jews—practice, worship, study, gather, and, yes, dispute as such—is infinitely more important than whether or not they actually descend from some long lost tribe of Israel. They are vastly "more Jewish" than Western Europeans or North Americans whose DNA may bear traces of Jewish ancestry but whose lived experience, individual sense of identity, religious practice, and group identification is anything but.

At this point readers should know with what kind of Jewish author they are dealing. In a word (or two): a diasporic Jew, an identity of which I became acutely conscious during several sojourns in Israel, as recounted in my *Zion in the Desert* (2007b). *Zion in the Desert* is what I call there an ethno-autobiography: exploring one's self through the study of one's ethnic peers. The "ethnic peers" to whom I was referring in that book were American Jews of Ashkenazi—that is, Eastern European—heritage. This designation infers, regardless of religiosity, a certain legacy of *Yiddishkeit*: the culture, language, and nostalgia retained from grandparents who had immigrated from "the Old Country." For many of the more assimilated Jews in the twenty-first century, outwardly this may mean little more than a yen for bagels and lox Sunday brunches and a familiarity with a smattering (many of them epithets) of Yiddish words. For others, including myself, it also includes memories of tight-knit and black-hat Orthodox Jewish communities in Brooklyn, a taste for gefilte fish and herring, and a gut response to klezmer and other music emanating from the old Yiddish world. I grew up with a certain Ashkenazi chauvinism (Long Island; Conservative synagogue) that associated these identity markers with what it meant to be Jewish. It was a wrong association. For none of this music, food, or language is part of the equally authentic Jewish culture and experience of, for example, Sephardic Jews elsewhere in the diaspora. Nor are they representative of Jewish culture writ large in Israel. Above all, none of it is an intrinsic element of Judaism, the religion and related life-cycle events that constitute, willy-nilly, the core of Jewish peoplehood.

This may be—should be—a banality to many readers. But it

dawned on me only after repeated interactions with Sephardim in the West Indies and Montreal and with new Jews in West Africa. Just as one can be culturally Ashkenazic (or Sephardic) and avowedly atheist, so one can be Jewish without any cultural reference or connection to either Ashkenazim or Sephardim. The Jubos, for instance, are very Jewish by religion, and still very African by culture: keep this in mind when Sar Habakkuk recounts the Jubo blessing over the kola nut. Their Africanness diminishes their Jewishness not a whit, no more than Americanness diminishes the Jewishness of Americans. It took a Jubo to get me to really appreciate this dialectic between religion and culture: "I think that one may not be able to get close to God if one deviates completely from his own background and culture," Remy Ilona told me in Abuja, the capital city in the middle of Nigeria. "Culture has Godliness in it."

Gatekeepers of Judaism should strive to appreciate this. Neither they nor other readers should be shocked or repulsed by the occasional invocations of prophesy, visions, and even witchcraft in the life stories of the Jubos. These are inescapable phenomena within the southern Nigerian milieu—just as they were commonplace among the early Hebrews in ancient Israel. The best exposition of this point of view is Howard Eilberg-Schwartz's 1990 book *The Savage in Judaism*. Or just read the Old Testament, particularly *Nevi'im* (The Prophets).

And so from earlier *ethno*-autobiography in *Zion in the Desert* I move here to *religio*-autobiography: exploring one's self through the study of one's co-religionists. This is the more challenging undertaking. Ethno-autobiography among American Jews who emigrated to Israel to found a kibbutz led me to define myself, ultimately, as a diasporic Jew; religio-autobiography among Nigerian Igbos has led me to question *why* I define myself as a Jew in the first place. Religio-autobiography, I submit, constitutes a greater challenge for most ethnic Jews than they are prepared to undertake.

I had originally intended to entitle this book *More Jewish in West Africa*. On the one hand, "more Jewish in West Africa" refers to the growing numbers of West Africans, many if not most Igbo, who are embracing normative Judaism and thereby making West Africa more Jewish than it is (or, depending on one's view of Jewish African history, making West Africa more Jewish than it has been in a long time). On the other hand, "more Jewish in West Africa" also refers to the ways in which, unbeknownst to them, my Igbo co-religionists have compelled me not only to feel more Jewish whilst amongst them but to question, back home in America, my own status as a semi-practicing Jew. It is in this vein that I ask the reader's indulgence when I toggle between the subjective and the scholarly. (Note to potential book reviewers: I am on to the "It is difficult to know for which kind of audience this book is intended" variety of criticism.)

I thank Markus Wiener for initially suggesting that I contribute my Jubo research to his fine imprint and Janet Stern for so skillfully improving the manuscript. Rabbi Wayne Franklin and Rabbi Joel Seltzer of Temple Emanu-El in Providence, Rhode Island, have been extraordinarily supportive of my commitments in West Africa, to communities Jewish and not. I again thank Rabbi Howard Gorin of Congregation Tikvat Israel in Rockville, Maryland, for introducing me to his friends ahd followers in Nigeria, and for sharing with me ever since his experiences, insights, and perspectives. It is for good reason that he is so admired and respected in Nigeria. Speaking at his synagogue on the Shabbat preceding his retirement was one of the greatest honors I have been extended. I did so with the blessing of his followers in Nigeria, to whom I owe my greatest debt.

CAC/IT/NO 23818

CORPORATE AFFAIRS COMMISSION
FEDERAL REPUBLIC OF NIGERIA

Certificate of Incorporation

of the Incorporated Trustees of

YOPHES JEWISH SYNAGOGUE

I hereby certify that

ELDER OVADIAH AGBAI, AZUKA PINCHAS OGBUKAA, BROTHER KINGSLEY YOSHIAH ANYIM, BRACHA EZE, GODWIN ARIEL NGENE,

the duly appointed Trustees of YOPHES JEWISH SYNAGOGUE have this day been registered as a corporate body, subject to the below mentioned conditions and directions.

Given under my hand and the Common Seal of the Corporate Affairs Commission at Abuja this Eighteenth day of May, 2007

CONDITIONS AND DIRECTIONS

This certificate is liable to cancellation should the objects or the rules of the body be changed without the previous consent in writing of the Registrar General or should the body at any time permit or condone any divergence from or breach of such objects and rules.

Note:

This certificate does not bestow upon the Organization the right to establish any institution, engage in any business and the like without permission from the appropriate authority.

114311

Optima · 51446 · 2/03 · F2426

Registrar - General

Nigerian government recognition of proposed synagogue

First Encounters with Jubos

Down the muddy, pot-holed, dirt path on the outskirts of Abuja our vehicle jounces, until we arrive at one of the least likely sights in this capital city, smack dab in the middle of Nigeria—a blue-and-white washed building with fading Hebrew characters painted on its outside walls. It is a warm, humid, late afternoon in December. One of my two companions is Abdulmalik Badamassi, a large, imposing royal from the tribe of Ibira. The other is another noble, Prince Azuka Ogbuka'a, a small, soft-spoken businessman whose mother tongue is Igbo. Abdulmalik, who works as a lawyer for the Nigerian government, is a Muslim but claims that "Ibira" is a corruption of "Ivri," or Hebrew, the "tribe" from which he originally descends. Azuka, for his part, has had a name change, and now goes by Pinchas ben Eliezer. The two did not know each other before I made plans to spend the holiday week of Hanukka in Abuja.[1] In fact, Abdulmalik, as educated and well-connected as he is, hadn't even known before I planned my arrival that there existed fellow Nigerians—in his own city, no less—who call themselves Jews.

---

[1] For a day-by-day account of that holiday encounter, see my "Among the 'Jubos' During the Festival of Lights," *Transition: An International Review* 105 (2011).

Entrance to Tikvat Israel, Abuja, Nigeria

From out of the building emerges a brown, full-bearded, middle-aged man who beams a broad smile and sports a colorful skullcap. "Shalom, Prof!" he greets me enthusiastically. "Welcome to Tikvat Israel!"

It is Sar Habakkuk, founder and leader of this unlikely Jewish community in Kubwa, Abuja. Perhaps even more unlikely is that his is not the only synagogue in Abuja—Pinchas will bring me tomorrow to his house of worship, Gihon, in Jikwoyi, on the complete opposite end of this sprawling metropolis. For the moment, though, we prepare to meet the rest of the excited, gathering congregation. For not only is this the eve of Shabbat, it is also Erev Hanukka.

If you are an MOT (Member of the [Jewish] Tribe)—or even just somewhat familiar with Africa—you undoubtedly know about the ancient Jews of Ethiopia, once referred to as Falashas. You may even have heard about the Abayudaya, a hundred-year-old community of Jews in Uganda. But "Jubos"? This is my term for the Igbos of Nigeria who have become, over the past two decades, the fastest growing community of Jewishly identified Africans on the entire continent.

Even before I first came to live in West Africa as a Peace Corps volunteer in the 1970s, Igbos were already commonly referred to as "the Jews of Africa," on account of their mobility, education, and business acumen. Then, the comparison was metaphoric. Now, Igbos are building synagogues, reading Torah, and teaching Hebrew prayers and songs to their children. But to the Jewish world, they are practically unknown.

That's because of a brewing, unresolved matter. Is the world—including their own government—prepared to recognize them as Jews?

* * *

With 160 million inhabitants, Nigeria has by far the largest population of any country in Africa. Thanks to its abundant oil reserves, it's likely that you fill your gas tank periodically with imports from its Niger Delta. (Nigeria is the fifth largest supplier of petroleum to the United States.) But for all its natural wealth and human capital, Nigeria is a troubled land.

Since its independence from Great Britain in 1960, Nigeria has known multiple coups d'état and experienced more years of military dictatorship than electoral democracy. It has also suffered the ravages of civil war. On the heels of the assassination of its prime minister and other top officials in 1967, the southeastern region attempted to secede under the name of Biafra. Despite aid from some foreign countries, including Israel, the revolt was crushed, and its people—mostly Igbo—justifiably feared genocide. (Igbos are the third largest of Nigeria's 250 "tribes.") The Niger Delta remains restive today, with private militias kidnapping oil workers and large-scale "bunkering": illegal siphoning off of black gold from the pipelines.

Over the past three decades religion has become an increasingly divisive force in Nigeria, rivaling tribalism and oil greed. When the British cobbled together their holdings in this part of West Africa in the early twentieth century, they cared little that the arid northern half of their colony was Muslim while most of the tropical southern portion adamantly rejected Islam. Over time, the animist south Christianized. Under the influence of American-style preaching, many southern Nigerians have become evangelicals, some even aggressive proselytizers. As for the most Muslim part of the country, since 1999 the twelve most northern of the nation's thirty-six states have adopted *sharia*, Islamic jurisprudence, as the law of the land. Even radical, violent jihadism has taken a foothold. The would-be underwear suicide bomber, Umar Farouk Abdul Mutallab, set off from his native Nigeria in attempt to explode himself over Detroit on Christmas Day in 2009. Two years later to the day, a group with the moniker "Western Education is Forbidden" (Boko Haram) killed scores of worshipers in suicide attacks on the national cathedral in Abuja and elsewhere. The Christmas 2011 bombings were the culmination of a campaign that had previously targeted political institutions in the northeast and in the capital: police command headquarters, the United Nations headquarters.

So who would chance thrusting themselves in the middle of this already polarized and voluble religious cauldron? The Jubos, of course.[2]

* * *

Edith Bruder, a French Jewish anthropologist, has written the most comprehensive overview of Jewish and judaizing communities in Africa today. In her 2008 book, *The Black Jews of Africa. History, Religion, Identity*, Dr. Bruder asserts the existence of twenty-five synagogues throughout Nigeria, and puts the high estimate of Igbo practitioners of Judaism at thirty thousand. Nigerian newspapers

---

[2] For a good treatment of the metaphorical incorporation of Jewish tropes within domestic Nigerian politics, see Milligan (2008).

publish figures in the forty thousand range (see, for example, Uwaezuoke 2011). Like many of the statistics related to ethnic groups in Nigeria, both numbers greatly overstate the reality. In any event, this is what Bruder says about their ancestry: "According to the Igbo lore of the Eri, Nri, and Ozubulu clans, Igbo groups traditionally claim descent from three particular Israelite tribes—Gad, Zevulun, and Menashe. . . . The interpretation of the Igbo name for the Supreme Being, Chukwu Abiama, is God of Abraham (*Chukwu* means God, and *Abiama* may be a derivative of Abraham)." Bruder relates the local belief that Igbos originated in "the place where sacrifices are made." Led by Chief Eri, they sailed down a tributary of the Niger River, settling in present day Iboland. By this account, "Igbo" derives from "Ibri," itself a transformation of "Ivri"—Hebrew. British colonial and missionary writers of the 1920s already were documenting the "Levite" practices of the Igbos, Bruder shows. It is a claim that some Igbo intellectuals had themselves made long before (Equiano 1789; Horton 1868), and that others have continued to make, particularly in light of the Biafran "holocaust," belief in a shared divine mission, and identification with both ancient and modern Israel (Ikeanyibe 1999; Alaezi 1999; Ogbukagu 2001).

But back at Tikvat Israel, on the outskirts of Abuja, Habakkuk is more preoccupied with ensuring the future of the Jubos as a community than proving the authenticity of their ancestral origins. After making Kiddush with Manischewitz wine (available in the local market at the equivalent of fifty dollars a bottle), and lighting Hanukka candles on a menorah consisting of painted Coke bottles mounted on a wooden frame, the man who looks like a sun-baked version of an Old Testament prophet beseeches me for just one thing—a Hebrew school teacher.

"We need a Jewish school to educate our children, because we know that Hebrew language is the key to the soul of the Jews. We can easily build the structure, we have room to board the teacher. All we want are lecturers, that's all. . . . Ours is a striving community, and we feel proud to be part of the Jewish heritage and people . . .

"There is a saying that 'One should not wear the garment of bashfulness in order to acquire knowledge.' So we have removed the vests of bashfulness, and ask that you inform our brothers over there [in America] that we need teachers to lecture our children on the rules and regulations of Judaism, our inheritance."

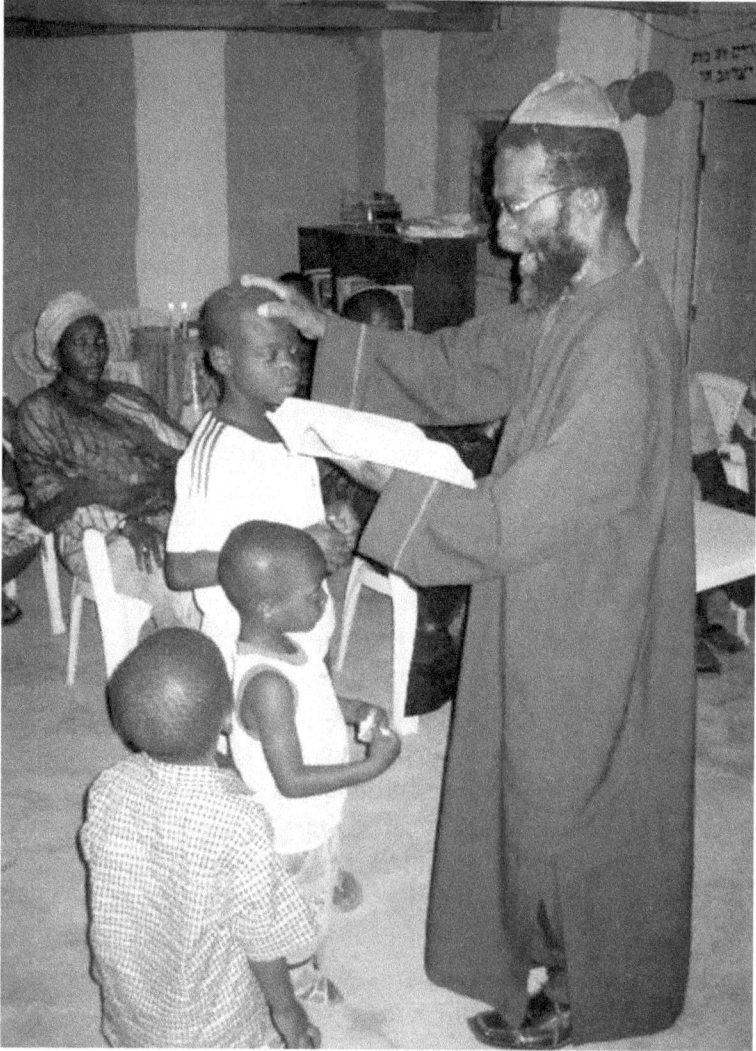

Habakkuk blessing the children for Shabbat

Other Jubos give a more sobering explanation of the need for a Jewish day school. "Our children can only attend school with Christian children. Sometimes they are beaten by classmates, because they do not pray to Jesus. It is very hard for them. We have"—and here I hear echoes of my father's generation, as they struggled as a Jewish minority in America—"a problem with assimilation."

Jubo children encounter daily contradiction. "They study with the Gentiles. When they come home, they pray in the name of Hashem. When they go to school, they train them to pray in the name of Jesus. It is wrong. My children don't follow them. But they used to have misunderstanding with their teachers. As far as the Torah is concerned, none of their teachers can stand [up to?] them. Even my small, little girl—she challenges her teacher, with Torah. But a child doesn't know how to challenge the way that an adult would. Not fall into their trap. If it is me, I would use ideas. The child will just challenge openly. And then the teacher rises and gets angry. And when a teacher gets angry with you, you never feel fine again in that classroom. That is why I am praying for a Hebrew teacher. Let us start, even with one."

Part of the problem is the local incongruity of being both Nigerian and Jewish. Resolving tensions between Muslims and Christians has been a challenge to successive governments of Nigeria since independence. One strategy is to subsidize overseas religious pilgrimages for each of the major faith groups—Mecca for Muslims, the Holy Land (Israel) for Christians. But what about the Jubos who yearn to pray in Yerushalayim (Jerusalem)? Without government recognition, they are precluded from similar pilgrimage privileges—unless they "pass" as Christians. Under these circumstances, imagine convincing a local Nigerian zoning official to grant a permit for a synagogue.

Now imagine being told that you're not even Jewish, because your foreskin was not removed according to Talmudic specifications.

* * *

For how long would having a Hebrew teacher suffice? As the community develops, its felt need for a resident rabbi is becoming more acute. Two types of life-cycle events impinge: death and marriage.

"We don't have a Jewish cemetery in Abuja yet," I am told when I inquire. "That's why we're talking about having a resident rabbi. Traditionally, Igbos don't bury their people outside their homes. They take their dead to their home, to their roots." The final resting place can be in the courtyard, even inside the house itself. Old people usually indicate where they wish to be buried ahead of time, although it is the responsibility of the senior member of the deceased's family to provide the burial place. "There is no marker, but people know where the elders are buried. Sometimes, they will plant trees of a particular leaf—*ogilisi*—that does not die."

As of yet, there is no Igbo *hevra kedusha* (Jewish burial society). But the time will come when Jubos will be placing stones on the graves of their departed rather than placing their departed alongside the stones in their yards.

With respect to weddings, I don't have to inquire: a certain Moshe ben Moshe seeks me out about his son, Baruch ben Moshe. Baruch, who is from Moshe's southern hometown of Nwerri, is betrothed to Ekwutosi of Zaria, in the north. The date is not yet fixed but preferably will occur four months hence. Ekwutosi is prepared to convert—but who can convert her? And, more pressing, who can officiate over the wedding? The nearest rabbi in Africa, I first think, is in South Africa—three thousand miles away. But then I remember: there is an ordained rabbi to the east, Gershom Sizomu, in Uganda, "only" eighteen hundred miles away. (For sure, it's a much tougher trip than Abuja-Johannesburg.) Then I wonder: Are there any rabbis left "up north," on the other side of the Sahara, in Morocco or in Tunisia? (That, it turns out, is even farther away than Uganda.) The geographic calculations become dizzying, the conclusion identical: when you're a Jew in Nigeria, and you need a rabbi, you've got a long way to go.

The Jewish wedding bind is a fairly new phenomenon in Abuja: the first one in Abuja took place on December 18, 2007, when

Moshe ben Levi married Ruth bat Yakov.[3] Before then, adults tended to find (or "rediscover") Judaism after they were already married. But now a new generation of Jubos has arisen, born and raised as Jews: there is greater expectation that they marry in proper Jewish weddings, complete with officiating rabbi.

The pressure is coming more from the female side: Igbo girls demand weddings. If a Jewish wedding cannot be arranged, a young Igbo woman will demand an alternative one. "It's a growing concern. If we don't continue to marry" in a Jewish manner, observes an elder, "we won't be able to prosper" as a community.

Many prospective brides of the community are not yet Jewish. "We elders ask the girl, we invite her" to become Jewish. If she agrees, she takes an oath. But vigilance is necessary, lest she "agree today and divert tomorrow." What if she changes her mind after the wedding? "We will chase her from the home."

In the meantime, how do they cope without a rabbi? "Wedding prayers are in the *siddur* [Hebrew: prayer book]. We recite them in Hebrew, under the *huppa* [Hebrew: wedding canopy]. We improvise. We see on the Internet."

* * *

Before entering Tikvat Israel for prayer, we shoo off from the hood of our car a goat that has curled up to take a late siesta. The rafters of Tikvat Israel are not filled, the wooden benches are hard, but the *ruach*, the spirit, for Kabbalat Shabbat is robust. Men and women sit together and sing exuberantly in Igbo-inflected Hebrew. We are led in prayer by two Jubo prodigies—Natan, a sweet-singing, gentle-souled man in his early twenties, and Hezekiah, a serious-looking eleven-year-old with the full-throated voice of a future *chazzan* [Hebrew: cantor]. The prayer books are familiar,

---

[3] I cannot confirm it, but I am told that the first Jubo wedding in Nigeria occurred in Enugu State in 1998, when Shalomith, daughter of early Jewish community leader Yerimahu Nwokeabia, was married to the son of Udambekee, another early community leader. They have since had a boy, Mordechai, and a girl, Hadassah.

Praying from photocopied siddur

Jewish prayer by flashlight

well-worn editions I have used in Conservative synagogues on Long Island and in Rhode Island. That's because the mentor of Tikvat Israel—indeed, he who modestly bears the title of Chief Rabbi of Nigeria—is Rabbi Howard Gorin, spiritual leader of the Conservative congregation in Rockville, Maryland, from which the Kubwa synagogue takes its name.

Rabbi Gorin pioneered American Jewish outreach to the Jubos in 2003, after news of his presiding over the *bet din* conversion of Abayudaya in Uganda spread and he received an invitation from Nigeria. It was not an easy trip—his expected contact at the airport did not show up, he fell ill from unfamiliar food and water, and he had to navigate the shoals of Jewish politics Nigeria-style. Still, he came away profoundly impressed by the knowledge, passion, commitment, and resiliency of this budding community of Africans yearning for Jewish learning. "They need encouragement," says the Maryland *melamed* (teacher), cautioning that the challenges of assisting the Jews of Nigeria (in education, community development, entrepreneurship) are considerable. But American Jews should also realize that the Jubos represent a unique "opportunity to develop one of the biggest Jewish communities in the diaspora."

"They believe they are descended from Israelites," Rabbi Gorin goes on, maintaining a studied agnosticism about his own views on their actual origins. "They practice circumcision on the eighth day, and they blow the ram's horn." Proof of Hebraic ancestry or mere cultural coincidence? Rabbi Gorin isn't saying. But what does it matter? Bottom line is that, among some of the 25 to 40 million Igbos of Nigeria, the rabbi detects genuine *neshuma*—Jewish soul. When pressed to quantify those who practice "normative Judaism" in Nigeria—Judaism as recognized elsewhere in the world, completely shorn of "Messianic" excrescence—he won't go beyond the low thousands.

Remy Ilona, Jubo attorney and author, is more categorical about Jubo origins. In his various publications, including *The Igbos: Jews in Africa* and *Introduction to the Chronicles of Igbo-Israel*, Ilona provides detailed analogies between Omenana—traditional Igbo customs—and ancient Hebrew practice. "Jewish history is Igbo history," he writes. "The Igbos are included among the descendants of the twelve sons of Jacob, . . . part of the very people that were forged in iron at Sinai." But Ilona is more active as a publicist for the Jubos internationally than as a regular participant in their ordinary community endeavors.

I meet Remy in his modest but book-rich house in the outlying Kuje Local Government Area of Abuja Federal Territory. (Out of tribal sensitivity, in the early 1980s Nigeria moved its capital from coastal Lagos in the Christian south to the more ethnically neutral center of the country.) Remy, gaunt and grinning, is suffering. He has recently undergone a hernia operation in Maidugari, in the extreme northeast of the country. It was a surgical procedure that saved his life, and some of its burdensome cost was underwritten by a Jewish benefactor. Through Kulanu, an organization that supports Jewish communities in the Third World, he still manages to raise the profile of Nigerian Jewry.

"Maybe it is a sign that I should be more involved religiously," he offers, suppressing his post-operative pain. At the end of my *bikkur holim* (visiting the ill), I present his family with a menorah, candles and, to his young niece, a dreidel. "Shalom!" he responds, in farewell greeting.

In Remy Ilona's library

Remy Ilona's writings do not highlight the problematic path that most Jubos have taken to arrive at their modern faith. It is not a simple Igbo-return-to-Hebrew-roots story. Brought up as Protestant or Roman Catholic, as most Igbos now are, a number of them first explored several alternative paths. Some were seduced into "Messianic Judaism" by an American-based pamphleteer and Internet evangelist. To be Jewish, they believed, was to follow the one Jew known best the world over—Yeshu, or Jesus. Slowly, after some years of worshiping this Jewish "son of God," some began to have creeping doubts. Prince Azuka Ogbuka'a was one of them, though his questioning began earlier than most.

"My father—a retired inspector of education—is the ruling Obi of the Abala kingdom in Delta State. He raised us as a traditional Christian family. [As a youth] I asked him, 'Father, we are Christians. The center of our worship, Christ, was a Jew. Why is it that most Jews I have read about are not Christians?'" Azuka's father had no answer.

Although Prince Azuka continued worshiping as a Christian, he kept raising questions and, spiritually restless, kept changing churches. In 1998 he left Anglicanism to become Born Again— "to be sure to go to heaven," as his companions assured him. But the Prince still had questions. "You say the Christian Shabbat is Sunday," he would challenge his Christian fellows. "Who decided it, and why? On whose authority?" The dogmatism of the responses grated on him all the more. They told him that you can't get all the answers if you want to go to heaven. Prince Azuka played along, but with increasing restiveness.

Next he joined the Seventh Day Adventists because of his "urge to keep the commandments as instructed." Introduced to pamphlets and books of the Messianic movement, he started to keep the Sabbath on Saturdays, on his own, at home. But he couldn't shake his mounting discomfort with Christianity. The Prince would lie awake at night, sleepless on account of his spiritual confusion. His religious conflict became a source of marital discord. Finally, in 2001, he met a kindred spiritual wanderer, who joined him in his worship at home. "What we're doing in Messianism is not the whole thing," his friend confided. "We have to continue searching." Together, they discovered the Gihon synagogue (officially, the Gihon Hebrew Research Centre).

Entrance to Orthodox synagogue

"In Gihon, I was taught the shema,"[4] says the fifty-four-year-old Prince Abuka—who now prefers going by Pinchas ben Eliezer—with great relief. "When you recite shema, you are actually saying, 'It's all Hashem, and Hashem alone.'"[5] At Gihon, the "elder" (no ordained rabbi yet presides) taught the princely Pinchas the difference between monotheism and polytheism. "You don't believe in that One God, and also in another Savior," as Christians do. For him now, the notion that a flesh-and-blood man may also be God is an absurdity.

"From then on," he continues, "I've not looked back. As I study Torah, I see the relationship between it and things we practice in our traditional culture—circumcision, New Moon, respect for elders. Great attention and care for widows and orphans. Leaving the corners of our farms for the less privileged. As I studied, I began to see how all these things are intertwined."

Spiritually, Pinchas is completely fulfilled as a Jew. But he is not alone in having paid a heavy price for his decision to become a Jew. Like several Jubo men I interviewed, his religious choice triggered ongoing separation from his wife. It visibly pains him.

"But what joy!" he bounces back, thinking of his family life. "Some months ago, I had the opportunity to bring my two sons— Joshua and David—with me to synagogue. My daughter Chidima also came."

How does Chidima translate from Igbo to English, I ask?

"'Hashem is good,'" Pinchas replies.

When Pinchas takes me to his synagogue, I think of the familiar Ashkenazi adage, "Two Jews, three synagogues." It is a jocular reference to the self-acknowledged Jewish tendency to fracture on account of disagreement about ritual or personality.[6] If Tikvat Israel

---

[4] As mentioned in note 3 in the introductory chapter, the shema [Hebrew: hear] is the quintessential prayer of Judaism.

[5] Since Jews are proscribed from uttering the actual name of God (or even trying to, since the true pronunciation is said to be unknown), the euphemism "The Name" (ha-shem, in Hebrew) is used, particularly in Orthodox quarters.

[6] In Abuja, at least, there is a geographic rationale: from the center of town, each is around a forty-five minute drive, in opposite directions.

is Conservative in orientation, Gihon Hebrew Research Centre is Abuja's version of Orthodox Judaism. There is a *mechitza* [Hebrew: partition] behind which the women (some with babies strapped to their backs) pray. The prayer books are Rabbi Schehr Artscroll editions, used back home in Orthodox *shuls* (synagogues). There is greater attention to ritual—including the fetching Jubo custom of in-between service hand-washing outside the walls of the synagogue. Gihon's larger congregation accounts perhaps for the synagogue's more prosperous appearance—finished ceiling and floors, enclosed book cases, individual chairs. It also possesses that for which Tikvat Israel yearns—a scroll from which the Five Books of Moses are chanted.

Orthodoxy in Gihon gives rise to the kind of disputation that would make any Orthodox community proud. I am responsible for one such problem (and politely refuse to resolve it). Because of my Friday afternoon interviews, we are delayed in lighting candles, both for Hanukka but especially for Shabbat. Not *so* late—it is 6:55 pm, only 15 minutes beyond the previous evening's officially designated time for Hanukka lighting. But Moshe the Cantor is

Ify and friends in the women's section of Gihon congregation

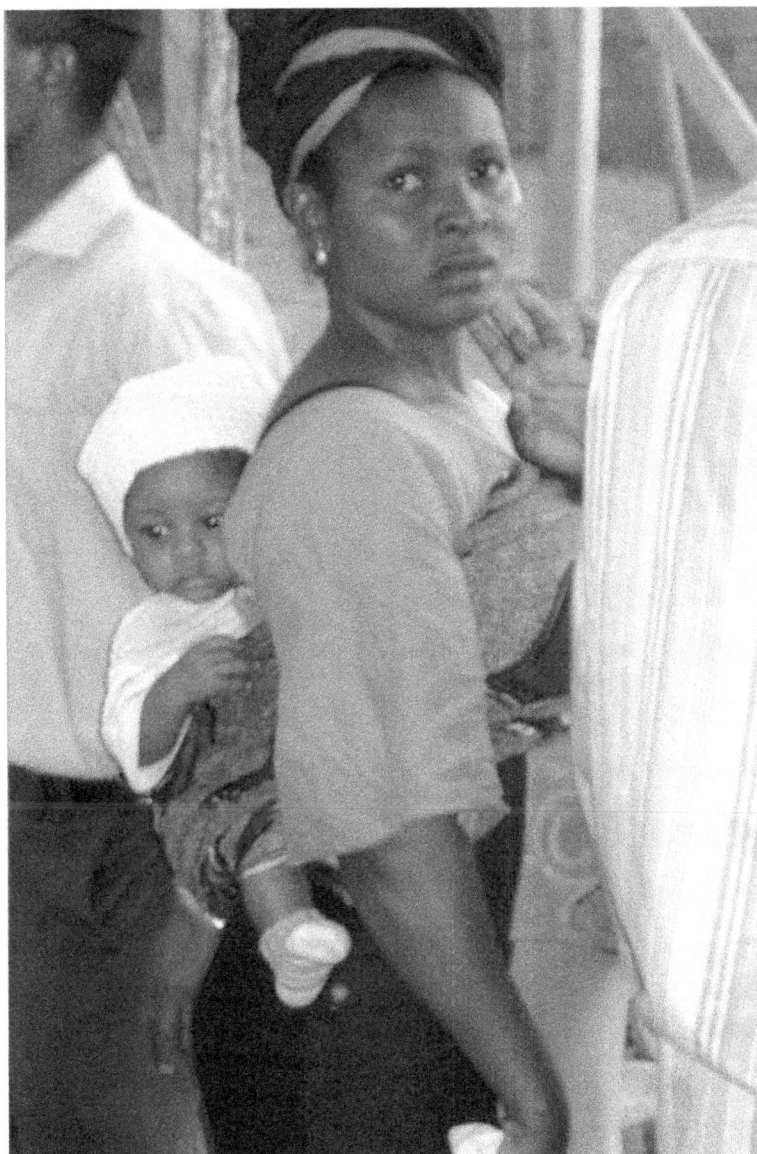

Bringing the young to shul

Ablutions before Jewish prayer

emphatic that it is too late, too dark already. They turn to me for a ruling.

"As I told you when I arrived," I respond feebly, referring to this first Judaic trip to Abuja, "I'm not a rabbi. I'm just a Jew. I defer to the rabbi of the community." But of course, there is no actual rabbi . . . Then another Jubo chimes in:

"Is it too late for me to light candles when I get home? I left at 3:00 pm, when it was much too early, and I haven't been back home, since." This triggers another line of halachic debating. More Jew than 'bo, no?

The interlude of halachic debating must have given Moshe time to figure a way out: "There is no way that I will strike a match," he at last declaims, in an authoritative voice. "I just won't do it." Then comes the Talmudic-style of compromise. "Only if I take light from elsewhere," and he gestures to the *ner tamid*—the Eternal Light (here, a kerosene lamp)—that flickers above the ark of the Torah.

Moshe climbs on a chair to reach the Eternal Kerosene Light. "Make sure it doesn't go out," another Jubo warns apprehensively, as Moshe carefully lifts the glass bulb of the lantern and tilts the frame to gain access to the little wick. So he winds up lighting all the holiday candles, Hanukka and Shabbat, in that requisite order, without striking a single post-sundown match, but in the process generating all sorts of Jewish ritualistic questioning.

That the ner tamid here is a lantern powered by burning kerosene is but one reminder that we are in Abuja in Nigeria, not in Boston or Brooklyn. Another is that bidding for the honor of coming up to and blessing the Torah (*aliya*) is conducted in Nigerian naira. If you glance out the window while rising for the *amidah* (the silent, standing prayer) you see goats chomping at vegetation poking up between the detritus thrown out from the surrounding hovels. And when you exit the synagogue, you are hit by the odors of underdevelopment—smoke from wood-burning stoves, decomposing waste, roaming ruminants with funky hides. No wonder, perhaps, that the services—an oasis for the nose as well as the soul—last so long.

Gihon neighborhood

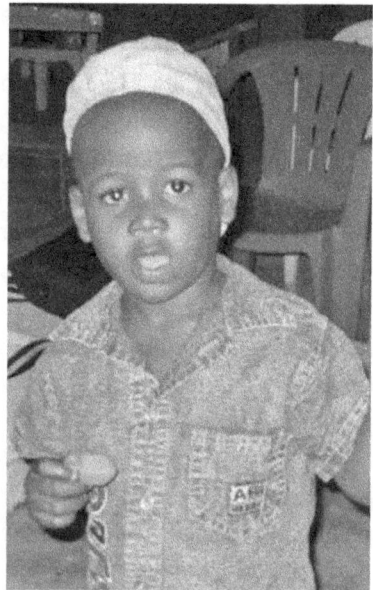

Hanukka celebrants

Hanukka comes to Nigeria

Hanukka menorah from Coke bottles

Hanukka celebrants

Deceased member of Gihon

* * *

Shabbat lunch study at the synagogue shows how much easier it is for Jubos to connect to Torah than it is for most Amjews (American Jews). Thanks to Rabbi Gorin's online study guide *Shalom, Africa*, photocopies of which are distributed, there is a solid basis for discussing the portion of the week. I happen to attend on Shabbat *Vayeshev* ("[And Jacob] dwelt").

It is a Torah portion chockfull of drama, emotion, divination, and sexual tension. Joseph prophesies from dream, is thrown into a pit by his jealous brothers, and is sold as a slave to Pharaoh. He resists seduction by Pharoah's wife, is imprisoned out of spite, and interprets more dreams from the dungeon. There is a curious episode about a serial widowed and long childless woman, Tamar, who eventually seduces her father-in-law on account of the refusal of her brother-in-law to impregnate her. For most Amjews and other "modern" Jews, these events are from a completely other

time and dimension. But here? Contemporary Jubo sensibilities
provide easier identification with aspects of the Old Testament than
do modern Ashkenazic ones.[7]

* * *

What kind of prayer services reflect the true essence of Judaism?
It is a question that splits Jewish congregations worldwide into
ever infinite variations of *tefilla* [Hebrew: prayer]. As the Jubo
community grows, and even begins to modestly thrive, tensions
inevitably arise between form and substance, between community
and *kavanah* [Hebrew: spiritual intent], and between Jubo haves
and Jubo have-nots. In many cities around the world without a
large synagogue but with a sizeable Jewish community, hotel space
is often rented for the High Holidays. In Abuja, Nigeria's capital,
such an idea has been floated, so as to accommodate all worshipers
under a single roof. How does Sar Habakkuk, leader of the modest
Tikvat Israel congregation on the outskirts of Abjua, react to the
suggestion that the Nicon Hotel be used for such a purpose?

"Yom Kippur is not a feast for pleasure. We are asking for forgiveness of our sins from our God, the Holy One in Israel. In this
synagogue, we pack all the chairs and sit on the floor until the end
of Yom Kippur.

---

[7] As the life stories in chapter three bear out, dreams have played an important
role in the process of bringing Igbos to Judaism. Igbo culture is not unique in this
regard: elsewhere (1993), I have explored the significance of dreams in modern
Hausa culture. More recently (2008) I have also shared some of my own West
Africa dreams, including one that revealed the unconscious fusion of the Africanist and Jewish parts of my brain. It is in this vein that I share the dream—a night-
mare, actually—which I had the night before the bar mitzvah guests (see chapter
two) were to return to Ogidi: *They are lined up, along a banco wall. I know that
they are going to be deported, Nazi-like, and that a bus will come and transport
them away. But I walk away to attend to some other matter for a short time. When
I return to the assembly point, they are all gone—not even the slightest trace of
the Jews of Ogidi is left. A wave of immense regret washes over me: I have abandoned the Jubos in the moment of their greatest travail.*

Perhaps Dr. Caliben's real-life invocation at the bar mitzvah of survival for
the Igbo and Jewish people triggered this anxious nocturnal event.

.

"I feel that going to a hotel—to stay in a high hotel, one of the highest hotels of Nigeria, and paying for accommodation there—is not right. Imagine, we have to contribute money, to pay, to be allowed there. A place where presidents are used to coming. If it is a festival for enjoyment, than we can do. But Yom Kippur? No, no, no, no. My spirit does not accept that.

"There is just no place in that hotel made for a poor man. Even the garden. Even the garden is furnished. If you don't have a private car to take you there, you have to hire a drop. I don't think that Hashem will accept this.

"I ask this question, 'What is Yom Kippur?' Will I go there and celebrate Yom Kippur without my family? I can't leave my family here and go there with my *tallit* and *siddur* [Hebrew: prayer shawl and prayer book] to celebrate Yom Kippur in the high hotel while my family remains here.

"That is my own opinion. I think it is better for me to go out into the bush [and pray], where sun and cold and rain will beat me because of my sins. I accept that more than to go to the hotel. Up in the mountain I have an open shrine where I can go and pray." It is just one of the places where Habakkuk meditates about being a Jew, about his relationship with Hashem. A place on a hilltop to pray on Yom Kippur. I shall envision this place when I receive my synagogue entrance ticket for the next High Holidays.

But not only on the High Holidays. I shall come to think of Habakkuk every time I wake up on Saturday morning in America and wonder: "What time is it in Nigeria? Where in the Shabbat liturgy are the congregants in Habakkuk's synagogue? And those who are *davening* (praying) in Gihon?" As the sun over Saturday on eastern standard time advances, I shall periodically wonder, thinking of the ceremony marking the end of Shabbat, "Have they performed *havdala* in Abuja yet?" For the Jubos put me, as a Jew, to shame; periodically, the thought will even propel me to shul.

They live more Jewishly than most Jews do in America. References to Torah and Jewish ethics are sprinkled in routine conversation. ("I don't want to do *lashon hara*," says one Jubo, invoking the Jewish interdiction against gossip as the subject of conversation

turns to others in the community.) Men don *kippot* when entering
their homes; some wear their *tzitzit* (ritual fringes) in public. Their
services are full, complete, in Hebrew, and daily. Their life, planning, aspirations, and achievements center around Judaism.

* * *

At the end of a quiet, tree-lined lane in this otherwise busy, dusty
city—on a street named for a Scottish missionary woman who put
an end to the custom of killing newborn twins, regarded as "be-
witched"—are armed guards who man a checkpoint outside a non-
descript house with high walls and towering antennas. Only when
you are searched, cleared, and announced may you approach close
enough to make out the discrete plaque on the front wall. This is
the embassy of the State of Israel to the Federal Republic of Nigeria.

Ambassador Moshe Ram is a career diplomat who nevertheless
finds working in Nigeria somewhat odd. "They don't function like
in foreign ministries in other countries," sighs the open-collared but
meticulous diplomat. "At times, it can be quite frustrating." Ambassador Ram's time is divided between promoting trade between
the Jewish state and Nigeria and countering the propaganda of Islamic fundamentalists littering the freewheeling local press. He has
little time left over to devote to the interests or concerns of what
other skeptics might uncharitably characterize as wannabe Jews,
Third World denizens desperate for Israeli citizenship.

The embassy is but the most formidable bastion of the Jewish
state in the Giant of Africa. There are also hundreds, if not thousands, of Israelis working in the construction industry, living in self-
contained compounds complete with chapels and rabbis. There are
American Jews living there, too, such as Thomas Timberg, Ph.D.,
the Orthodox consultant for the World Bank, with whom I light
candles on the sixth night of Hanukka. Tom hosts Jubos at his
hotel home for Shabbat from time to time. He even provides some
Judaic employment, "pay[ing] a group of [Jubo] congregants to
build a *sukkah*" (a booth for the Feast of Tabernacles) in the
appointed season.

There is also the seventy-year-old Teddy Luttwak (elder brother of famous D.C. neocon Edward, a young survivor from Transylvania) who has fashioned most of his post-Holocaust career in Africa selling marble fixtures. Irrepressible Teddy (a citizen of Italy) married a Nigerian lass three decades his junior and is the doting first-time father of a boisterous boy just starting out in a primary school. Over a sumptuous dinner Teddy asks—as if I were a wandering *yeshiva bocher* (young man studying at Talmudic school) visiting an old country *shtetl* (Jewish village)—if he might hire me to give his young son Hebrew lessons.

But few of these other Jews, regardless of how many years they've lived in Nigeria, know all that much about their local, would-be co-religionists. Nor do they wish to. When I ask a source close to the Israeli embassy to explain its general lack of interest in the Jubos, I'm told that "the last thing [the embassy] needs is for some crazy rabbi to fly over from Israel, convert them, and declare that they are Jews." There are four or five times the number of Igbos in Nigeria as there are Jews in Israel. For sure, only a tiny percentage of them currently affirm a Jewish ancestry. But what if a rabbinic decision obligated the Jewish state to confer the Right of Return upon all Jubos? Economic incentives to emigrate, it is feared, would drive millions of Nigerians to convert.[8]

Yet none of the Jubos I meet speaks of moving to Israel. To visit Zion, yes, but not to live there. And here's the rub: because theirs is not recognized by the Nigerian authorities as a bona fide religious community, Jubos do not get the kinds of subsidies that Muslims receive to go to Mecca, and Christians do to visit Jerusalem. So, in order to go on pilgrimage to Israel, several Jubos have had to "pass" as Christians.

Under such conditions, merely obtaining a building permit for a new synagogue structure becomes an exercise in theological exegesis and identity politics. Read how this plays out on the ground in Nigeria's capital:

---

[8] "Every Igbo man is a Jew," one prominent Jubo informs me, "but the consciousness is not there." Only in half jest does he refer to eastern Nigeria as "the home of fifty million lapsed Jews."

"In a government office I met this gentleman when I was [seeking] a piece of land for a new synagogue. He showed me the district. There was an area marked for the police station, an area marked for fire service, an area marked for parks, for a neighborhood center. Then we shifted to another district. There was an area marked for mosque, for church. The same thing that is here is duplicated there—mosque, church, fire service, police, and so forth. So I said to the gentleman, 'But you people are not being fair to us.'

'What do you mean?'

'Where is the synagogue?'

'What is a synagogue?'

I said, 'Ah ah! My friend, I know you have your first degree in town planning. You have your second degree, your masters, in urban and regional planning. Now, you are an assistant director. You have toured all over the world. And yet you don't know what a synagogue is?'

'Ibiakwa!' he answered in Igbo. (It means, 'Here you come again with your jokes.') 'I know. A synagogue belongs to the Jews. Is that not where they pray?'

'So,' I said, 'why did you first ask me what a synagogue is, since you know?'

'Where are the Jews?'

'Here you see one, standing before you!' I told him. 'Look at me. There are many of us that you don't know. We are Nigerians. We deserve equal treatment and equal rights. It is an act of apartheid. You don't treat us as equals. You recognize the Christians, you recognize the Muslims, but you forgot about the Jews.' I went further.

'My friend, the next district you are planning, make a provision for a synagogue. It's important, very, very important. Have the Jews in mind. We are here! If not, we will write to the National Assembly. We will begin to complain.' I impressed it upon him. 'Somebody has to start it.'"

FEDERAL CAPITAL TERRITORY, ABUJA

APPLICATION FOR GRANT/REGRANT OF A STATUTORY RIGHT OF OCCUPANCY
ACKNOWLEDGEMENT

FILE NUMBER: *MISC 79268* DATA ENTRY DATE: *04/07/07*

This is to acknowledge the receipt of original application for Grant/Regrant of Statutory Right of Occupancy
with the following particulars:

Date of Application: *17/04/07*
Name of Applicant: *YOPHES JEWISH SYNAGOGUE*
Address of Applicant: *FLAT 203, F C D A SENIOR STAFF QUARTERS, JABI, ABUJA*
Purpose: *RELIGIOUS*
State of Origin:

The following documents were received or checked.

	ITEMS SUBMITTED OR REVIEWED
PROCESSING FEE PAYMENT SLIP	YES
TWO PASSPORT SIZE PHOTOGRAPHS	
TAX CLEARANCE CERTIFICATE	
COPY OF NATIONAL ID CARD	
COPY OF BIRTH CERTIFICATE/AGE DECLARATION	
COPY OF INTERNATIONAL PASSPORT	
COPY OF C-OF-O OR R-OF-O FOR PREVIOUS ALLOCATION	YES
LETTER OF ENDORSEMENT FROM THE MINISTRY OF FOREIGN AFFAIRS	
BUSINESS REGISTRATION CERTIFICATE	
ENVIRONMENTAL IMPACT ANALYSIS REPORT	
MEMORANDUM AND ARTICLES OF ASSOCIATION	
PROJECT FEASIBILITY STUDIES	
PARTICULARS OF DIRECTORS	
CERTIFICATE OF INCORPORATION	YES

Signature ——————————— Date: 04/07/07

For Minister
Federal Capital Territory

Disclaimer
This acknowledgement does not in anyway validate the authenticity of the documents described above. All documents
are subject to further verification for authenticity.

This acknowledgement must be presented at the time of collection of Letter of offer of Grant. Please notify us of
any change of contact address or any other vital information contained in your original application. Contact us directly at:

ABUJA GEOGRAPHIC INFORMATION SYSTEMS OFFICE: 9 KUMASI CRESCENT, WUSE II, ABUJA, NIGERIA
09-6716100, 09-6716200, 09-6716300, 09-6716400, 09-4132356, 09-4132357
recertification@abujagis.com info@abujagis.com http://www.abujagis.com

THIS ACKNOWLEDGEMENT CANNOT BE SOLD OR TRANSFERRED

Application for new synagogue occupancy

APPLICATION FORM FOR INCORPORATION OF TRUSTTEES

URE "A"
AND OBJECTS OF THE APPLICANT BODY

S/N	AIMS/OBJECTS
1.	Teaching and spreading teh Light of Torah (Commandments of God)
2.	Spreading an destablishing peace between man and men
3.	Training teachers of Torah (commandments of God)
4.	Carrying out acts of Charity to Mankind
5.	Establishing Shalom (peace on Earth)
6.	To orgainze prayer meetings, prayer conferences, camps and conduct prayer sessions on any matter at any place and for any period.

ENCLOSURE "B"
RULES AND REGULATIONS GOVERNING THE BODY

A) The Trustee of____ YOPHES JEWISH SYNAGOGUE

for the purpose of the Companies and Allied Matters Act No. 1 of 1999, Part C shall be appointed at a General Meeting by two-third majority votes of members present.

B) Such Trustees (hereinafter referred to as "The Trustees") shall be 5 in number and shall be known as THE REGISTERED TRUSTEES OF_ YOPHES JEWISH SYNAGOGUE

C). The Trustees may hold office for life but shall cease to hold office if he:-

(i). Resigns his office

(ii). Ceases to be a member of the registered Trustees of YOPHES JEWISH SYNAGOGUE

(iii). Becomes insane

(iv). Is officially declared bankrupt

(v). Convicted of a criminal offence involving dishonesty by a court or tribunal of competent jurisdiction.

(vi). Is recommended for removal from office by a board of Governors and Trustees majority vote of members present at any General Meeting of YOPHES JEWISH SYNAGOGUE

Or

(vii).Ceases to reside in Nigeria

D) Upon a vacancy occurring in the number of trustees, a General Meeting will be held to appoint Another eligible member of ____ YOPHES JEWISH SYNAGOGUE

E). The trustees shall have a common seal.

F). Such common seal will be kept in the custody of the Secretary (or whoever is desired) who shall produce it when required for use by the Trustees.

G). All documents to be executed by the Trustees shall be signed by such of them and sealed with the common seal.

H). An auditors(s) shall be appointed at the general meeting to audit the accounts of the organisation Annually

N/B:THIS ENCLOSURE SHOULD BE INCORPORATED INTO THE CONSTITUTION OF THE ORGANIZATION

Purposes of proposed Yophes synagogue

* * *

Who is a Jew? The question ties all sorts of Jews in knots, creating great discord within "a people" that supposedly considers itself as one. Orthodox Jews reject converts from the Conservative and Reform movements. Israeli rabbis are increasingly suspicious of the status of American Jews, even of Orthodox provenance. In such a world, Jubos have a long way to go before receiving widespread recognition as Jews—even though they practice Judaism more consistently, punctiliously, and earnestly than do, say, the president, prime minister, or most ambassadors of the Jewish state itself. Remarkably, the Jubos don't seem to mind about outside approval, so secure are they in their Jewish faith and identity. So Jewish are they, in fact, so self-confident in their Judaism, that they care remarkably little what the (dominantly white) Jewish world at large thinks about them—even if they acknowledge that "when Jews from outside provide materials of encouragement, they are saying, 'We are with you.' That inspires us to do more. It is helpful. We are not alone."

Still, echoes of the fracture within world Judaism are beginning to wend their way into West Africa. They even feed into the synagogue politics, if not rivalries, to which African Jews are no more immune than are Ashkenazic or Sephardic ones. The case of the controversial and polarizing Rabbi U. serves as an example.[9] "Jonathan," a prominent Jubo, recalls the incident:

"I received a call from this rabbi."

Rabbi U. had been living in Israel but was then based in a north-

---

[9] Although a journalist from Israel is reputed to have published full names and details emanating from his own on-the-ground investigation of the controversial rabbi, in deference to my hosts' sensitivities I prefer to preserve in anonymity the identities of persons involved in this story. I here dub the teller of this tale Jonathan, exemplar of loyalty (to the future King David) in the first book of Samuel.

ern city in the United Kingdom.[10] "He said he heard that I had hosted another rabbi, and asked if it was so." It was. "He then told me he would come to Abuja. He expected me to wait for him at the airport. So I hired a car.[11]

"On the way from the airport he asked me, 'Where do you belong?'"

It was a question that both confused the rabbi's host and made him ill at ease. Jonathan asked his guest to put it to him again. The question had nothing to do with residential location or social identity, and so Jonathan again asked what the rabbi meant. Rabbi U. responded by inquiring about the previous rabbi who had visited before repeating, "Where do you belong?" It was all about denominational affiliation.

"It is true that the rabbi I hosted before is Conservative," replied Jonathan, referring to Rabbi Howard Gorin. "I admire him. I respect him. I have accepted him as my teacher, and I cannot go against him."

"I cannot go your synagogue," Rabbi U. informed Jonathan, "if it is a Conservative one."

In recalling the encounter, Jonathan asked me why there is "violence" among rabbis. But to Rabbi U., at the time, he asked, "Is there divination in Israel? Did God not create one people?"

"It could cause trouble with my people," the Israeli rabbi from Britain answered him. To which Jonathan replied, "I don't want trouble with my people."

"So I left him off at the junction," Jonathan continued in his retelling. "Elder A. met us there. Rabbi U. transferred all his things—books, suitcase, Sefer Torah—from the taxi to Elder A.'s car." The three of them wound up at Elder A.'s house. "There the

---

[10] As are the overwhelming majority of rabbis ordained in Israel, he was Orthodox; non-Orthodox denominations have a relatively small presence in Israel and struggle for recognition by the government and for legitimacy in the eyes of the people. As the old saw goes: Secular Jews in Israel will admit, with varying degrees of pride, that they don't ever go to synagogue. But the synagogue that they don't attend, they assert defensively, in repudiation of "suspect" variations, has to be Orthodox.

[11] As with most Nigerians, relatively few Jubos own cars.

rabbi handed me the Sefer Torah, and I danced with it. But to this day I have not returned to A.'s house." This was just the beginning of the discord that the uninvited rabbi began to sow.[12]

"Rabbi R. had sent materials to the East [of Nigeria], to C., for distribution to the [Jewish] community. But C. refused to release them. The Rabbi sent people to C.'s place. But he continued to refuse. He just wanted to keep it all for himself. It was like what we say in Igbo: 'Can you take the goat out of the mouth of the lion?'"

C. was the leader of the Jews in his locality. He didn't like the competition from this rabbi from overseas, and the challenge to C.'s authority that this represented. So he went to the police, and even the security services, and claimed that Rabbi U. was actually a spy, an agent for the Mossad. He had come to destabilize Nigeria by relaunching a bid for Biafran independence. Thus was Rabbi U. arrested and deported. But his pronouncements have not been forgotten: "Only the light of Torah," he is remembered as declaring, "can break the cloud of darkness over Nigeria."[13]

The saga of Rabbi U.'s visit to Nigeria from England is reminiscent of the story of Shalomith, a Jubo woman with a son in Great Britain.[14] Both speak to the Jubos' coming to terms, compassionately and with forbearance, with the "white Jewish" world's difficulty in embracing them as brethren.

Shalomith was blatantly rejected by members of a congregation in London. "Who is your rabbi?" they demanded. "What is your synagogue?" Rather than renounce the xenophobic Jewish enterprise *in toto*, she followed the interim advice of a Jubo elder to join a Messianic congregation in England and accept as her greater mission bringing these other religious searchers towards "Orthodox" (i.e., normative) Judaism.

How patient the Jubos are with the skeptical Askhenazi world. How understanding they are of our insularity, fears, hypocrisy, and

---

[12] The following paragraphs combine multiple accounts of what happened next, all of which corroborated each other.

[13] His rhetorical questions are also recalled: "What kind of country is this? What kind of Judaism is this?"

[14] See the life story of Kate (Shalomith) Chukuma in chapter three.

prejudice. Are Amjews—so eager to embrace a secular Jerry Seinfeld as a "Member of the Tribe"—as ready to accept a pious Jubo as one of their own?

Who are the truer Jews—the Seinfelds or the Jubos? Who, really, are the more open-minded ones?

* * *

It is hard enough to assert Jewish identity as a Nigerian. It becomes even harder when compatriots with no interest in becoming Jewish nevertheless embrace Jewish mysticism. Yes, there is even a move to bring Kabbalah to Nigeria. Pinchas recounts a meeting that was held at a fancy Abuja hotel.

"A gentleman came in from the U.K. and they hosted a meeting of the Rosicrucian Order at the Hilton. They spent a lot of money—close to fifteen million naira. Those of us who were involved paid ten thousand each to host other people so that they could come.

"As of now, the Kabbalah Center has sent in a huge number of volumes of the *Zohar*[15]—no translation, no transcription. In my presence, at that meeting, a retired civil servant donated two million naira for its distribution.

"'Incidentally,' I said, 'this *Zohar* is written in Aramaic. What will you do with it?'" Instructions from the Kabbalah Center had it that, even without the ability to read the *Zohar*, fixing one's eyes upon the pages would be beneficial.

"Since you have coopted us," Pinchas said to the Rosicrucians, "it would be better to find some Jewish communities for distribution" of the *Zohar*. Better that the Jewish communities come first, he reasoned, instead of these things finding their way into the hands of non-Jews.

"So, just the other day, four cartons went to Oweri. A copy has

---

[15] Sourcebook of Kabbalah, the *Zohar*, written in the Aramaic language, dates to the thirteenth century (although some believe the claim of its medieval rabbinic annotator that it actually was composed in the second century by Rabbi Shimon bar Yochai).

come to Gihon. Copies are going to twelve communities in Delta, one to Enugu, and one to Habakkuk.

"In our ignorance, some ten years ago, you could hardly find anyone who was praying in Hebrew. Today, in Gihon, many people are praying in Hebrew, using siddur. Twenty years ago, you could hardly find a copy of the siddur, anywhere. Today, there is no community that doesn't have siddur," all sorts of editions. Just as "today we have someone who can read Hebrew, tomorrow we will have someone who can read Aramaic. 'Like senior brother and junior brother.'"

But it is not just the *Zohar* in Aramaic that intrigues Gentiles of Nigeria about Judaism. As the Rosicrucian meeting progressed, Pinchas says he also learned of plans to obtain a Torah scroll. He asked one of the Order's local representatives, a civil servant, if he knew what the Torah really was. The Nigerian Rosicrucian answered to the best of his knowledge.

"Do you know," Pinchas retorted, "that you cannot have Sefer Torah in a place where you don't have at least a minyan to pray? You can't have Sefer Torah without Jewish prayer being said. That is un-Jewish. Do you have a minyan to say Jewish prayer there?" The man said that he didn't understand what Pinchas was talking about. Pinchas continued his line of questioning.

"Do you have the intention of building a synagogue?" The man confessed ignorance. "So what is the definition of the Kabbalah Center? What is it going to look like?"

Pinchas counts on the Rosicrucians to keep him informed of their plans. In the meantime, he does his best to preserve the authenticity of Judaism in Nigeria.

* * *

Hanukka is ending, and the time has come to bid adieu to the Jubos. Hardest of all is taking leave of Hezekiah, the prodigal boy cantor at Tikvat Israel. A skinny preteen with precociously penetrating eyes, Hezekiah regularly leads prayers in brilliant Hebrew. Although timid and soft-spoken in speech, as *chazzan* his beautiful

Hezekiah leading evening prayers

and full-throated chanting sails far beyond the unfinished rafters of this Igbo *shteibel* [Yiddish: tiny synagogue].

His eyes brimming with hope, this future African Hasid looks up at me and asks, in his young, earnest voice, "Will you come to my bar mitzvah?" His request sears my soul.

As for Abdulmalik, the Muslim lawyer who met me at the airport—last I heard, he is taking lessons in Hebrew and Torah from Iheanacho Onyekwe, that is, Moshe ben Natan Levi, the self-taught, mellifluous cantor and religious school teacher at the Gihon synagogue.

Only in Nigeria. And only on account of the Jews.

CHAPTER TWO

A Bar Mitzvah in Abuja

Two-and-a-half years after my initial encounter over Hanukka with the Jubos of Abuja, eleven-year-old Hezekiah's poignant request was still ringing in my ears: "Will you come to my bar mitzvah?" His question joined poignancy and naïveté: how could he have any idea of what a transcontinental, Boston-to-Abuja journey actually entails? In none of my subsequent communications with his father, Sar Habakkuk, did the question of (much less a date for) Hezekiah's bar mitzvah ever come up. I nevertheless made plans to return to Nigeria in August 2011 and bought a plane ticket for Abuja. I telephoned Habakkuk to announce my intentions.

Was the phone line that bad? Had I so lost familiarity with Habakkuk's accent? Might I have involuntarily slighted the man? I could have sworn Habakkuk was saying—even after I asked him to repeat himself, "That is bad, Sah [Sir]. That is bad."

That is indeed what he said.

But what was "bad" was not my volition to come back to Abuja and see him and his family, but my announced dates of arrival and departure. "The twenty-third of Av," Habakkuk went on, invoking the Hebrew calendar, "is Hezekiah's bar mitzvah. We checked— that is the Hebrew date of his birthday. I think it is also the twenty-third of August."

This information threw me for a loop on several counts. To begin with, rare is the Jew—even the religiously observant one—whose primary reference for time, outside the context of marking religious holidays, is the sixteen hundred-year-old lunar calendar. Not even the holiest of rabbis, I daresay, remembers that his appointment with the dentist is for 3:00 pm on the third day of the week on the 22nd of Tevet rather than on Tuesday, January 17. The Hebrew calendar is not the most user-friendly calendar (at least not for solar-oriented folk), what with its 354 days and the periodic need (seven times in every nineteen-year cycle) to add a whole extra month so as not to be completely out of whack with the sun and its attendant seasons. For sure, certain months have a familiar ring: Av (because the 9th of it, Tisha B'Av, marks the destruction of the Temple in Jerusalem); Shevat (because the literal name for the Jewish Arbor Day is the 15th of it [Tu B'Shvat]); and Nissan (for some Jews, because the Passover seder always begins on its 14th; for me, because my first car was a Japanese model of the same name). But Iyyar? Cheshvan? That the 23rd of the month in 2011 corresponded with both August and Av was mere coincidence, one that, given Habakkuk's uncertainty, would require double-checking. If correct, it would also require KLM rerouting, rebooking, and hefty date-change fees. Bar mitzvah in Abuja? Not a peep about it before, and now I'm in jeopardy of just missing it.

Another calendric conundrum: it is customary to celebrate bar mitzvah on Shabbat, Saturday, the Jewish Sabbath, when the Torah is read and the young man is called up to recite (at a minimum) the blessing over its reading. But it is perfectly permissible to do so on a Monday or a Thursday, days on which the Torah is also ritually read.

August/Av 23 fell on a Tuesday.

I called up Rabbi Gorin, the Baltimore-based "Chief Rabbi of Nigeria" who was also receiving a late summer invitation to the bar mitzvah in Abuja. He sighed. "It's exactly the kind of thing that drives me *meshuga* [Yiddish: crazy] there, and why I'm reluctant to get too involved. They do things at the last minute. And sometimes not according to *halacha* [Hebrew: Jewish law]. They have their own ways, but I don't want to be seen as condemning them. On the other hand, if I participate in a bar mitzvah on a Tuesday, with Torah-reading, it's as if I'm endorsing a contravention of Jewish law. I can't do that. And since I'm viewed as the Chief Rabbi, I can't go there in a 'private capacity,' either, just to attend." Poor Rabbi Gorin, tied up in knots as he tries to do good by the Jubos . . .

I, on the other hand—as I reminded my Jubo friends when I was asked to weigh in on a point of Jewish law two years before—"am just a Jew." My participation would have no bearing on the Jewish legitimacy of what they do. Tuesday or not, I would be at that bar mitzvah.

There are only a couple of KLM flights a week out of Abuja, the least onerous way to get to and from Abuja from Boston. I would change my return ticket, out of Abuja instead of Kano, for Wednesday, August 24.

But in the meantime, Habakkuk lays another unexpected Jewish trip on me, one whose baggage is more psychological than Samsonite. "I want to buy tarpaulin," I hear him say. "How much does it cost?"

I ask him to repeat. He does so. Again, I wonder why in the world he is asking me to shlep tarpaulin to Africa. For shelter, so as to conduct the bar mitzvah outdoors? Does he realize how much space tarpaulin takes up in a suitcase?

"Three of them," he goes on, startling me now into a vision of excess baggage that precludes my ability to pack even some pairs of socks. "Three of them. One for Hezekiah. One for my brother. And one for myself. How much does one cost?" Only then did I realize that my earnest Jewish friend in Abuja was inquiring—and confusing me, by stressing the first syllable rather than the second—not about **tar**paulin but rather te**fill**in. Thus was I forced to deal with my longstanding phylactery allergy.

* * *

I had long been allergic to tefillin, those quintessentially exotic objects of Jewish prayer ritual. No, let me put it frankly: placing and tying those weird-looking boxes and whip-esque leather straps on my arms and forehead had, over time, come to feel outright repugnant. But now my encounters with Nigerian Judaism were making me into an agent and enabler of those very same bizarreries.

"Take to heart these instructions," God tells His people, first according to the thirteenth chapter of Exodus and then elaborated upon in the sixth chapter of Deuteronomy. Love and obey Me unconditionally, He says. Tell your children to do so, too. And, as a reminder, "Bind these words as a sign on your hand, and let them serve as a frontlet between your eyes."

Now who, hearing the word for the first time in history, and with no other set of instructions (much less a design sketch), would know what on earth "frontlet" is supposed to mean? But leave it to the Jews (or at least the Pharisees) to figure it out. "Frontlet," as the Almighty's will was divined, turns out to be a two-inch square black box containing four compartments, each with a folded parchment of hand-written Mosaic verses, and black leather straps hanging from two sides. The box is supposed to sit on the hairline, each strand of the strap hanging over a shoulder. As for the hand sign— this is a similar box (but without separate compartments), containing a single parchment of the four verses in Hebrew. Its strap is longer than the frontlet's and single-stranded, so that it can wrap around the arm seven times, then do an additional loop-de-doop three times around the middle finger, and then wind a couple of times more around the hand, before it is finally tucked in at the palm. If those rope-a-dope instructions sound more complicated than the hardest knot in an Eagle Scout's kit, imagine that you're a twelve-year-old already overwhelmed with anxiety about chanting publicly from a non-Roman script in a foreign tongue in an atonal mode. No wonder that most Jewish boys drop the morning tefillin routine (daily, except for the Sabbath and holidays) after their bar mitzvah.

Even as a semi-practicing Jew, in the decades following my bar mitzvah two words would come to mind whenever I'd see a coreligionist don those strange instruments of prayer ritual: "bizarre" and "primitive." The black box protruding from the temple (usually framed by a white prayer shawl draped on the head) looked alternately fearsome, frightening, or monstrous. After being mortified about sado-masochism and its related paraphernalia of kink, those leather straps wound around an upper limb even seemed vaguely pornographic. What could better fit the anti-Semitic stereotype of the Jew as an incomprehensible alien than the bizarre ritual with the little black boxes and dangling leather straps? And what other ritual so reminded me of the primitive origins (let's not forget the animal sacrifices and blood sprinkling) of my ancestors? The very sight of tefillin became increasingly repulsive to me, especially when hanging from a Jewish head.

Encounters with "Mitzvah Mobiles"—vans or booths from which ultra-Orthodox but otherwise amiable and outgoing emissaries of the Chabad movement approach Jews on the street to perform the tefillin commandment—used to leave me bemused, and even occasionally compliant. But a six-month sojourn in Jerusalem inoculated me entirely from tefillin entrapment.

My tipping point came at the Western Wall, the most revered location in Judaism. On the male side (women must be segregated at the Wall; the sight of a woman praying alongside men—much less donning tefillin—can start a riot), ultra-Orthodox regulars amiably offer to help you lay on the boxes and strap on the leather. Just like the Chabadniks. And they look like the Chabadniks, too—black hats, coats and beards, white shirts and shawls. But then, in the course of helping you perform the mitzvah, they ask for money. Persistently. Insistently. Not for themselves, at least not ostensibly, but for "the needy." But you soon realize—or you should—that they are "needy" Jews, too.

There is a Yiddish word that even many assimilated American Jews know—*schnorrer*. It means beggar, or moocher, and it carries connotations of both familism and obnoxiousness. There is another relevant Yiddish word, but this one is used only in Israel: I picked it up during that same sabbatical in the Holy Land. A *freier* is a naïf, a sucker. Among wise-guy *sabras* (native-born Israelis), freier is one of the most derisive things you can call someone.

I resolved not to be a freier. And I came to associate donning tefillin upon request with being a freier.

I don't recall how it came up, but in Jerusalem I once discussed my tefillin allergy with an Orthodox (but modern) Brooklyn-bred Israeli friend of mind. Yossi understood completely—but then went Jew-jitsu on me: "That's *precisely* why I like putting on tefillin," he said. "*Because* it looks, and feels, so primitive. It's what gives me a physical connection to this ancient tradition of ours."

On one level I understood. But not on the affective level. Reveling in our primitivism?

When Habakkuk asked me over the phone for the price of tefillin, I had absolutely no idea—no more than I had known the price of a Torah scroll, until he asked me for that information during my initial Hanukka in Nigeria. So, despite my phylacteryphobia, I felt obligated to contact my rabbi, once again, to get a price estimate on the premium exotica of Judaism.

The answer—this being Judaism—came in the form of unanticipated questions. Was the arm box for a right-handed Jew, or a lefty? Did the prospective tefillin-wearer prefer his leather straps to be shiny or dull? (Dull, it turns out, is costlier.) Would the worshiper be satisfied with a basement quality of ritual object to fulfill the Mosaic commandment—starting at around two hundred dollars—or did he want a higher-end set of parchment-in-a-box? There *was*, however, a definitive answer to one related question that Habakkuk's query had triggered: there is no used market for phylacteries.

I was stunned to learn the price of these little allergies of mine. My thoughts went back to the iconic immigrant story of an eager Old Country Jew tossing his tefillin overboard during his passage to the New World/New York, so as to symbolize and seal his break with the past. I thought of that story again a few months later when, in the garage clutter of boxes to be discarded pending the house move of an elderly aunt, I came across a serviceable pair, about to be junked along with other belongings of her deceased husband unclaimed by immediate family members. But for now, I was just beginning to dig deeper into my tefillin conundrum: becoming the provider of an object that I personally found antipathetic.

But how could I not honor the earnest request of Jubos eager to observe Judaism as scrupulously as circumstances permit? How could I transport tefillin all the way to Nigeria without recalling how to actually use them? And what if *I* was expected to teach Hezekiah how to put them on? The pressure attendant on this bar mitzvah was unlike that of any other I had prepared to attend.

If the price of tefillin threw me for a loop, it gave Habakkuk great pause. When I broke the news to him on the phone, he told me that he would, in that case, purchase just two pair. Then I received a rare e-mail from him. In it, he confirmed the date of the bar mitzvah ("23rd of AV5771 or 23rd August, 2011") and explained why he could now afford only one pair:

"Because of this money that is involved, it will be too much for me. Igbo Jewish Community is coming with their Sefer Torah from Ogidi, Anambra State. And I will pay for their transport. [Cost for] the bus that will bring them and go back with them is 60,000 naira. So that is why I have decided to 'cut my coat to my size.'" If you convert sixty thousand Nigerian naira into Judaic dollar purchasing power, it comes out to the cost of two low-end pair of tefillin. The literal knots of tefillin were further metastasizing into guilt-inducing mental ones.

Shortly before I am to leave for Nigeria, Habakkuk informs me, over his ever crackling cell phone, that he has changed the date of the bar mitzvah. "You are not supposed to read the Torah on the weekday, except for Monday or Thursday," he has somehow discovered. Knowing how keen he had been to peg the bar mitzvah to his son's actually turning thirteen, I fear he has now postponed the ceremony until the following Thursday—that is, *after* my (now second) rebooked departure date. Bar mitzvah pressure mounts further.

Fortunately (for me, if not for halacha), Habakkuk has decided to move up the bar mitzvah date by one day, to Monday, the day before Hezekiah's actual thirteenth birthday. Is he stretching Jewish law on my account? It would be unlike him to do so, and I never want to know.

It was a relief to know I did not have to again rearrange my itin-
erary. But I still did not recall how to put on tefillin.

So just a few days before departure I found myself, as is not my
wont, at early morning *minyan* (prayer quorum), taking an urgent
refresher tefillin practicum from the rabbi. Rabbi Franklin had ordered in a new pair of tefillin for the bar mitzvah boy. But in one
of the pair of tefillin for his father (once belonging to my stepfa-
ther's father) we find a defect: the arm strap has torn and is therefore too short for adult use.

"You'll have to go to Brookline," Rabbi Franklin counsels. He
mentions the name of a Judaica shop. It is fifty miles away. But it
is the closest establishment where this specialized kind of work
can be done. "Ask for Eli. He'll be able to replace the strap. While
you're at it, you should probably also replace the strap for the *shel
rosh* [Hebrew: (tefillin) of the head]). And the *shel rosh* that *you'll*
be wearing needs adjustment, too." My clean-shaven, otherwise
modern rabbi is lending *me* a congregational pair of these remem-
ber-God devices from antiquity, so that I do not arrive ritualistically
empty-handed/headed. Gauging from the huge circumference of
the head strap of the loaned tefillin, the previous user must have
had a severe case of hydocephalus—during *shacharit* (morning
prayers), the frontlet kept slipping off my hairline, down onto my
brow, occasionally falling smack dab on the bridge of my nose. So
instead of having a mere practice session, I was now facing a full
tefillin tune-up.

As I hurtle up the stress-inducing Boston Expressway, all on account of these Hebraistic contraptions that I had rejected decades
before, I begin to pray—that Eli will actually be in!

My prayer is answered.

Eli projects the "classic" image of Jew: black skullcap, white
shirt, black pants, white skin, long beard. I don't risk upsetting the
operation by describing to him Habakkuk, the actual end user of
these tefillin-in-need-of-repair. (Is it permissible for the Orthodox
to facilitate the laying of tefillin on persons—let alone black
Africans—whom they do not consider halachically Jewish?) Eli is
sufficiently impressed to know that I am taking tefillin to Africa.

He even praises me: "Travels to Africa, thinks to pack his tefillin
. . ."

After some time in his workshop, Eli emerges with the re-
strapped *shel yad*. "Put it on," he tells me.

I begin to welcome the opportunity to rehearse my renewed
mastery of Jewish antiquity and manual dexterity, eager to show
the truly pious Eli that I too know the order and procedure of the
laying, tying, winding, unwinding, rewinding of straps and the accompanying *berachot* (blessings). But for Eli, we're there not for
devotion but for business. "Just try it on. Let's see how it fits." This
is more Moe Ginsburg, the once-famous New York City clothier,
than Mitzvah Mobile.

Only after I have completed the fifty-mile drive home do I realize I have forgotten to have Eli adjust the head strap for the
tefillin that *I* will be wearing at Hezekiah's bar mitzvah. I already
foresee that, *shvitzing* from the tropical heat, during services in
Abuja the tefillin will be slipping perilously towards my nose.

* * *

"Shalom, Sir! Professor, do you eego?" I ask Habakkuk to repeat.
Although I am now in Zaria to the north, fewer than 150 miles
away from his home, understanding Habakkuk on the cell phone
remains a challenge. "Do you eego?" I hear him ask again, this
time his voice obscured by some ruminant-like noise.

Tomorrow is the day I am to travel to helter-skelter Abuja and
the Habakkuk homestead. But for the moment I am staying with a
French linguist of African languages on the comfortable campus
of Ahmadu Bello University. The ABU campus is modern, the staff
housing comfortable: water runs from indoor taps, the ceiling fans
are spinning, the refrigerator is humming. On the other end of the
line, it sounds from the loud ambient bleating (is it sheep?) that
Habakkuk is calling me from a farm.

And then I realize . . . No, it is not a sheep that is bleating in the
background. Habakkuk has been asking me not "Do you eego?"
but "Do you eat goat?"

The bleating becomes louder. Habakkuk elaborates. "We are going to slaughter a goat." For the bar mitzvah feast, naturally. "Will you eat it?"

Thirty-two years prior, my father came to visit me at my school 160 miles north of Zaria, where I was serving in the Peace Corps over the border in Niger. As a gesture of hospitality, my fellow teachers offered him a kid goat, which in short order was turned into barbecue for the party in his honor. It was the only time during his visit that I saw my father—who had stopped eating red meat many years before—flinch. Back then, despite my father's discomfiture, I did enjoy the rare treat of grilled goat-on-a-spit. But now that I had myself renounced eating mammals, I better understood what Dad must have been feeling.

In a sense, it is touching for Habakkuk to ask if I will consume the animal before he goes ahead and slaughters it. From the previous visit he must have remembered my dietary quirks. But I also sense that, no matter how I respond, this goat that I have heard protesting so clearly over the cellular band width is doomed.

Have you ever been asked on a bar mitzvah invitation R.S.V.P. card if you would prefer "fish or chicken" for your entrée at the celebratory feast? This, I realize, was the Jubo bar mitzvah banquet equivalent.

* * *

I arrived overland at Habakkuk's home, later than I had wanted, on the afternoon before the bar mitzvah. Police checkpoints into the capital had become choke points: Boko Haram, a violent Islamist group, was wreaking havoc.[1] But I did arrive in time to witness an unprecedented event: the end-of-day arrival, by fifteen-seat minibus, of bar mitzvah guests from Ogidi, a full day's journey from the southeastern part of the country. One by one, fourteen Jewish Igbos—men, women, and children—piled out, fatigued but

---

[1] Two days after I leave Abuja, Boko Haram will send a suicide truck bomb into the United Nations headquarters there.

Torah and guests' transport

ebullient. The first Jubo out of the van cradled in his arms the fif-
teenth, most precious of the occupants from Ogidi: the Sefer Torah,
the Scroll of the Five Books of Moses, without which a kosher bar
mitzvah would not have been possible.[2]

Greetings among long separated kinsmen and family would
have to wait: as the light began to fade, the male guests from Ogidi
formed a joyous procession, singing and dancing as they accompanied the Sefer Torah into Tikvat Israel, the Habakkuk family synagogue. To spirited prayer and song in Igbo-inflected Hebrew, they
lovingly unwrapped the protective cloth from the casing of the
Torah, carefully standing it on the table reserved for this purpose.
The scroll itself would not be seen until the ceremony the following
morning, when its case would be opened at the appointed time. In
the meantime, the house guests had to be fed.

Habakkuk's homestead consists of two buildings. The principal

---

[2] Although most people think kosher means "acceptable for Jews to eat," its
broader meaning is fit, acceptable, or appropriate according to Jewish law and
custom. (See Rosten 2001: 189-193, for an even wider array of usages.)

entrance to the main structure opens to a receiving parlor, on whose walls hang framed portraits of Rabbi Howard Gorin and other Jewish guests from abroad. The parlor leads to Habakkuk's bedroom, which adjoins another bedroom, which adjoins yet another. Beyond that second adjoining bedroom is a small storage area for foodstuffs and kitchen supplies. The bathroom—the only inside room with an actual door—is just behind.

Habakkuk has given me his bedroom; in the first adjoining bedroom will sleep six women and children, and almost as many in the second adjoining room. Rooms are separated by light curtains. Instead of knocking, in order to announce my path to the bathroom I say, "Excuse." To which I am greeted, in response, by "Shalom, Sah." Or, if I must relieve myself in the early morning and on my way inadvertently wake family members from their slumber, they awake with a start and an automatic greeting of "*Boker Tov* [Hebrew: Good morning], Sah."

Somehow, Habakkuk and family manage to accommodate the fourteen other house guests. I ask him what it has been like to prepare the bar mitzvah from the beginning, what has gone into it.

"It's a very big occasion to me. Hezekiah is my only son and I have to do everything I can to assist him in this bar mitzvah. Because he is worthy of it. He is talented. He can read Hebrew. He understands everything in Hebrew. He is almost the best chazzan you can ever see [in Nigeria]. Let me say he is the second or third best chazzan here in Abuja. Even to the east, he is the second or third best chazzan.

"When a boy is trying to follow the customs of his father, then that boy deserves help. That is why I said I will do everything to celebrate this bar mitzvah. It is once, once in a life. What else can I do for him if I don't do it [right]?

"I have tried my best to equip him for his bar mitzvah. I got two suits for him. The only spiritual material I have is my old tallit, for him to make use of it for now. I called the people of Ogidi to [lend] me tefillin for the bar mitzvah, and also to come down with their Sefer Torah.

"Since last month I started arranging my home, because I know

I am going to have national guests and an international guest. Keeping the house in order, keeping the synagogue in order. So that when anyone enters, they know this is where we worship the Most High.

"I spent a lot of money to transport the Sefer Torah, the ark, back from the east down to this place. I hired a vehicle to bring them and taken them back. Sixty thousand naira. It is not a small [sum]. But this is what I can do to make sure that I fulfill this mitzvah for my son Hezekiah.

"I thank Hashem who assists me in everything. I am very happy that everything is over [i.e., prepared]. Hezekiah is prepared."

I ask Habakkuk if he intends to have me speak at the service.

"Well, of course. You have every right to speak. You are one of us. You are an elder. We learn from you, because you know more than us. We are learners."

"We are *all* learners," I correct him. "To be a Jew is to be a learner. The highest rabbi is a learner. The youngest boy is a learner."

"But the experience is of a different category," he counters. "You cannot compare the [learning] experience of a rabbi to that of a small boy."

"When do I give the gifts?" In addition to the tefillin and embroidered skullcap from my rabbi, I am giving Hezekiah a *yad* — a pointer (literally, "hand")—for reading Torah and my own bar mitzvah tallit.

"You should give the gifts in the presence of the congregation. And in his life he will never forget it."

After all of the uncertainty that changing the bar mitzvah day entailed, I can't help asking Habakkuk why he did it. "I had already made up my mind on the date of the bar mitzvah," he tells me, recalling it was going to be Tuesday, August 22, on Hezekiah's thirteenth birthday, the 22nd of Av according to the Jewish calendar. "But then I went further into study. And I read in a book that the ark should only be opened on a Monday or a Thursday (and, of course, on Shabbat). It is written that Moshe went to the mountain to bring the Torah on Monday, and came down on Thursday. That is why it is permitted to read the Torah on these two week days. The next is Shabbat. That is basic, because we must study Torah on that date. That is why I backdated the bar mitzvah. And," he added, having calculated the time between the end of the 22nd of Av (at dusk) and the beginning of the 23rd of August (at dawn), "the back date is not so much—only nine hours."

* * *

Amid the sound of roosters I awake the morning of the bar mitzvah to an even more unusual scene outside: from the glasses, bottle, and banter around a table near the synagogue, I can tell that Habakkuk and some overnight guests have already begun a kind of celebration. My host invites me to join them, pointing to the reddish edible on the table. "This is our tradition," he begins. Even without the presence of special guests, there is a daily thanking that goes on:

"We use this kola nut to thank the Almighty Father every early morning. We get out of bed and do the ritual of washing hands. Then we get the kola nut and give thanks to Hashem for being with you all the night and raising you [from sleep], alive, in the morning . . ."

"'Kola nut never hear English,'" he translates literally from the vernacular: the kola does not understand the English language. "It hears only the language of the people who make use of it—that is, Igbo language. Even if we wanted to bless the kola nut anywhere in this country, as far as the kola nut is concerned, we must speak the language that it understands. Because the kola nut hears!

"That is our tradition. That is why you meet us this morning, at this beautiful table, with this kola nut. We have already prayed, giving thanks to God for bringing my brothers from far away in the east, all the way to Abuja. For allowing them to sleep in peace and for raising them up. We praise God for His assistance to us.

"This is our tradition. You may now eat the kola nut. One man already said the prayer, and everyone else said 'Amen.'"

I put a piece of the bitter nut into my mouth and wash it down—

this is optional—with spirits from the bottle. It is strong! My companions guffaw at my grimace and whelp. But the nut business is serious.

"In Igboland," Habakkuk goes on, without kola nut, you cannot do anything—you cannot get married or even slaughter fowl." Nor, I am catching on, even celebrate a bar mitzvah.

* * *

Before changing into my bar mitzvah service clothes—black-and-gold robe and red cap, gifts from Habakkuk two years before—we go over the order of ceremony. I needn't worry about having to lead any part of the service myself: Jubo cantors are much more proficient as *shaliach tsibur* [Hebrew: "emissary of the community"; prayer leader] than I, and one of the Ogidi elders, Emanuel Ikegbunam, has accepted the honor of officiating over the service. Nor do I need to worry about the awkwardness of simultaneously worshiping and photographing: not only is weekday filming permissible by Jewish law, but Habakkuk has hired a professional videographer to record the service and festivities.

Before we enter the synagogue, Elder Ikegbunam asks that all assembled give their attention to Habakkuk, who in turn presents me as "a good friend, a brother, coming all the way from the United States" for the bar mitzvah of his son, Hezekiah. "Two years ago he started Hanukka with us here, and he finished Hanukka with us here. He brought a gift—it was the first time I saw Hanukka candles. He brought to us the candles, and *kippas* [Hebrew: yarmulkas, ritual skullcaps], from his teacher, Rabbi Franklin. It is my friend Rabbi Gorin who introduced him to me. I am very happy today that he is in our midst to celebrate the bar mitzvah of Hezekiah, the celebrant. I thank the Holy One of Israel who has assisted me to bring up my boy to be an active Jew." It is now my turn.

"Shalom," I begin.

"Shalom," the congregations responds.

"I bring greetings from Rabbi Franklin, my own rabbi, in America. He has given me a letter of congratulation to Hezekiah, which

I give to Hezekiah now. I also bring greetings from Rabbi Gorin, whom you know."

"Yes," the assembled respond in recognition.

"Today is a great day because of the bar mitzvah of Hezekiah. Today is Hezekiah's day!"

"Baruch Hashem!" respond the assembled.

"But who is Hezekiah?" I ask. "Well, the *first* Hezekiah was a king, the fourteenth king of Judah. He is remembered for making reforms that made the religion more pure. For example, at the time there were still some cults, Jewish cults, that worshiped idols, and King Hezekiah got rid of them.

"King Hezekiah is also remembered for bringing prosperity to the Kingdom of Judah. For example, he brought water to Jerusalem by engineering an underground tunnel of water. He is also remembered for building warehouses for storing food, and goods, and for increasing sheep." I pause.

"What about this Hezekiah, *our* Hezekiah? Is he a king? No. But I think he is already a prince . . ."

"Baruch Hashem," someone calls out.

"A *sar*," I go on, using the Hebrew word for prince, "a prince of Jewish prayer, as a chazzan , as he will show in our prayers shortly. He will also read Torah for the first time as a bar mitzvah."

"Yes!"

"And for this I wish to present him with a *yad*," at which point I address myself directly to the boy, "to hold while you read from the Sefer Torah, and to point to the holy words as you do so." These words are translated into Igbo but I hear the word "point" and "pointer" in the translation.

"Study, too, is so important to be a Jew. That is why I give you this book on Judaism, so that you study more, even in English."

"Baruch Hashem," calls out a congregant.

I read out my inscription on the front page: "'To Hezekiah, On Your Day of Bar Mitzvah—Because Study and Learning Are Always at the Heart of Judaism.' Is it not so?" I ask the Jubos around me.

"It is." The book is circulated. More commentary in Igbo.

"May you continue, Hezekiah," I go on, "to be a prince of *tefilla* [Hebrew: prayer]. And as with King Hezekiah of olden days, may your strengthening of Jewish practice also bring material prosperity to this community . . ."

"Amen!"

". . . of which you are today a man, according to Jewish teaching and tradition."

I have one opportunity to publicly share my Jewish philosophy in Igbo regalia, and so I take it.

"This is a Jewish community. It is also an Igbo community, isn't it?"

"It is."

"To Jewish religion you bring Igbo culture, just as Jewish communities around the world bring their particular cultures—from Europe, from America, from Morocco, from Egypt, from Algeria. That is why today I am happy and honored to wear this *isiago*"—the traditional robe—"and this *ubu*"—the red customary cap. "To show honor to the Igbo Jewish community of Nigeria which has raised you, Hezekiah, to this day of mitzvah.

"I say this because some people wonder, 'Why this white man wear Igbo costume'?" Laughter abounds around. "I have explained now, yes?"

"Yes, yes."

"Hezekiah," I continue, "with the permission of my mother, Helen, I give you my own bar mitzvah tallit, the one that she and my departed father, Samuel—in Hebrew, Shalom ben Aleksander, *zichrono l'vracha*—gave me for my own bar mitzvah. So when you wear it, you are wearing not only a part of me but also the spirit of my parents, Samuel and Helen."

"Shalom!" someone cries out. "Baruch Hashem!"

"Hezekiah," I conclude, "in the name of Rabbi Franklin I present you also with these tefillin . . ." Hezekiah is wide-eyed as he accepts, with both hands outstretched, the felt bag containing the brand-new phylacteries.

"Tefillin bind us to the mitzvot, yes?"

"Yes," he manages to utter.

"These tefillin will also bind you to the congregants of my synagogue, Temple Emanu-El in Providence, USA, as led by our Rabbi Franklin."

"Baruch Hashem!"

"I thank you for listening to me," I tell the congregation. I turn to Elder Ikegbunam. "I thank you for allowing me to speak."

Habakkuk turns to me. "On behalf of the Tikvat Yisrael, and Nigerian Jews, and the Ogidi Jewish community which has come all the way from Anambra State—we are giving thanks to you. May Hashem reward you . . ."

"Amen!"

". . . May he keep you for us . . ."

"Amen!"

". . . as you are one of us today. I remember what you said last time you were here: 'I am a member of this synagogue.' I remember that . . ."

"Baruch Hashem!"

"So we are also saying today, we are also members of your own synagogue!"

Applause. "Baruch Hashem!"

"May the Holy One of Israel, Blessed is He . . ."

"Blessed is He!"

". . . bless everybody who assists us. Rabbi Franklin—I have never known him before. I have never seen his face. But look how he's assisting us. May Hashem keep him for us!"

"Amen!"

"I know one, one day we will 'see together.' Baruch Hashem!"

"Baruch Hashem!"

"You are most welcome, Sir. *Todah rabbah*" [Hebrew: Thank you very much].

Before entering the synagogue I remove my red Igbo cap; under it I have been wearing an equally bright red yarmulke. Inside is stamped the name of some bat mitzvah celebrant from a suburban congregation in northeastern United States.

* * *

Elder Ikegbunam directs us to enter the synagogue, but not before two preliminary rituals: individual washing of the hands (with the requisite Hebrew blessing *al nitilat yadaim*) and private recitation of the meditation upon entering a house of prayer (*berov chasdecha ahvo vaytecha*). Most Jews throughout the world will recognize the former prayer only in the context of pre-meal purification; as for the latter, not even in ultra-Orthodox communities have I seen the faithful forming a line at the shul entrance and patiently waiting as each congregant first pauses at the threshold to recite the 52-word beseechment.

Once inside, yet another Emanuel—this one, son of Paniel and Hadassah—takes charge. It is he, another of the Ogidi contingent, who has been extended the honor of leading prayers. It is also he who—thank goodness—ably assists Hezekiah and Habakkuk in donning their new tefillin for the first time. I am surprised to learn later that this tall, strapping prayer leader attends high school.

Ablutions before prayers

Emanuel ben Paniel has brought his own tefillin from Ogidi (God knows where he obtained his), as has his father. I notice a strange detail in the wrapping around the fingers—the Ogidi Jews add a loop around the pinky. Another Jubo innovation? Is this kosher? Have I—so recently a phylacteryphobe myself—already become judgmental about tefillin wrapping style?

Services proceed as recognizable in any synagogue around the world—at least ones in which the services are conducted principally in Hebrew. There are no shortcuts in shacharit, and from time to time I have to ask Hezekiah, next to whom I am seated, where we are in the service. After an hour or so we arrive at the part of the service at which the Jewish boy, by being called up to the Torah scroll to bless and perhaps—as is the case with Hezekiah—to chant from it directly, is considered by the congregation to be a man.[3] This being a weekday, there are only three readings from the Torah: Hezekiah is called up third. He performs beautifully.

---

[3] Actually, according to Jewish law, a Jewish boy automatically becomes a bar mitzvah ("a Son of the Commandment"; that is, one bound by the commandments) when he turns thirteen.

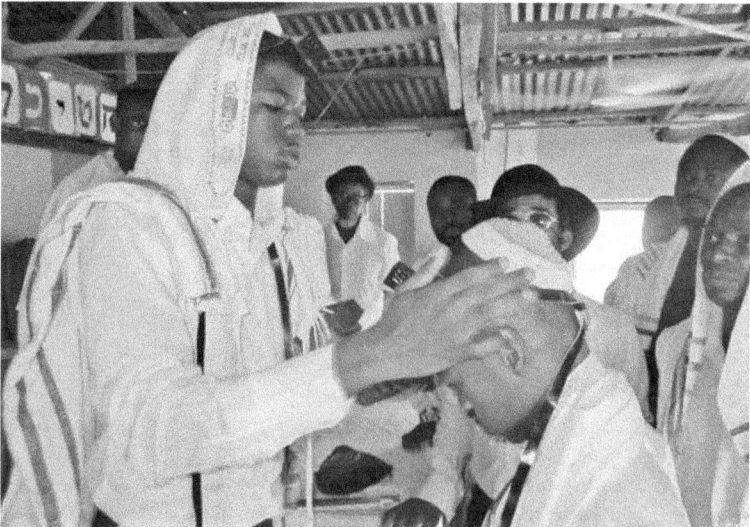

Hezekiah receiving blessing

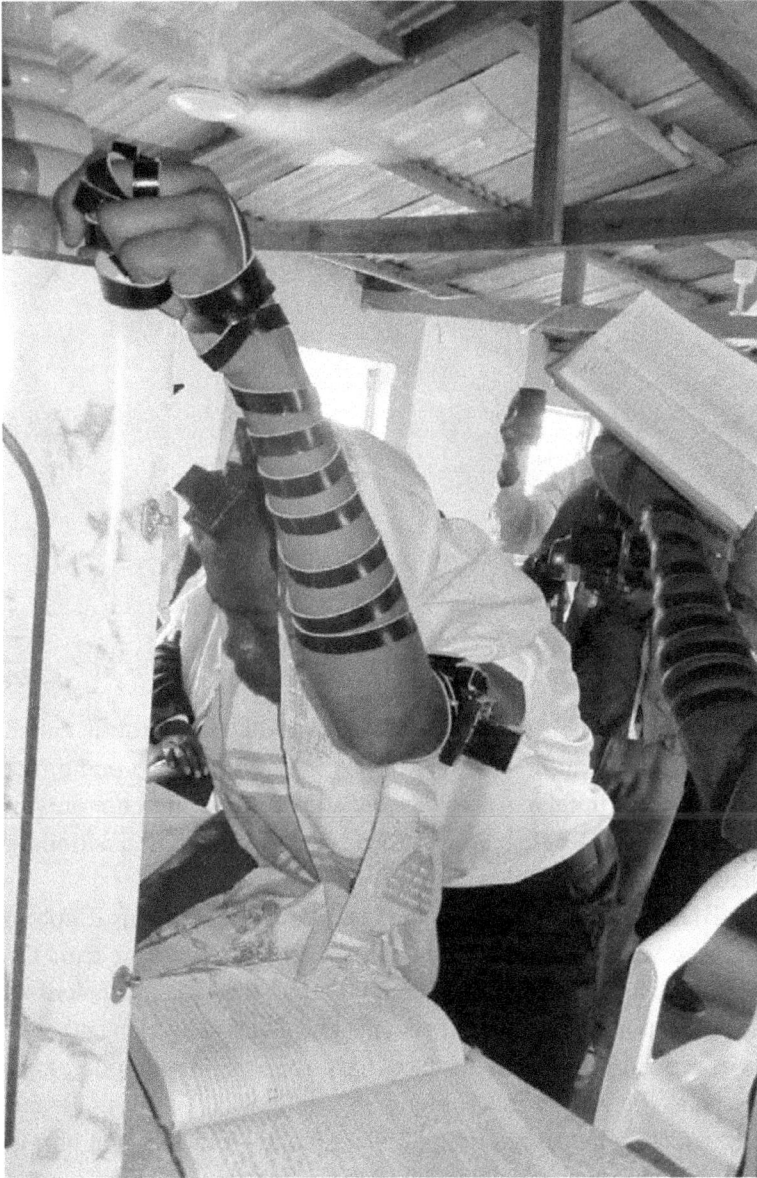

Hezekiah reading from Torah

Hezekiah in author's tallit

To mark his son's passage into adulthood, Habakkuk is called to recite the traditional prayer of paternal release. It is one of the few times during these services that a prayer is recited not only in Hebrew but in English as well. And it is a curious translation, at that:

"Blessed is He, Blessed is the One, You, Hashem, our Elhohim [Hebrew: God], Ruler of the Universe, Who has freed me from the punishment to this boy." The congregation, solemn, sober, serious up to that point, now erupts into song and dance. The men and boys twirl around the middle of the synagogue, arm-to-shoulder, endlessly, as the womenfolk look on, beaming. Hezekiah is not a natural dancer—by disposition, he is a scholar—but we rope him in to cutting loose as we do an Igbo version of the Israeli hora.

Eventually, it is time to return the Holy Scroll to its case.

"And this is the Torah!" the Law, intones Emanuel the cantor in

Hebrew. The congregation repeats in a collective shout, also in Hebrew, "This is the Torah!"

"that Moses set forth . . ." he goes on.

"That Moses set forth!" we repeat.

"before the children of Israel . . ."

"Before the children of Israel!"

"according to the commandment of the Lord . . ."

"According to the commandment of the Lord!"

". . . by the hand of Moses."

"By the hand of Moses."

As the service proceeds, the kids—Hezekiah's buddies—become all the more animated in their singing. The peak of prayer fervor comes with the shema ("Hear O Israel!") and the accompanying chorus, in Hebrew as always, "God Will Rule for Ever!" After more than two hours, the formal prayer service comes to an end.

Then come the formal meal blessings (kiddush) and invocations. Emanuel Ikegbunam takes over again, as the plastic white chairs of the synagogue are rearranged to face the kiddush table.

"You are welcome to the bar mitzvah of our young chazzan, Hezekiah ben Habakkuk. Today, you are all witnesses to the fact that he is a man—a full-fledged Igbo Jewish man. He can now join in forming the minyan. It is a very big step that he has taken today in his bid to live out and accomplish the divine mission to which the Almighty has called him. You can see that we come from far and near—north, south, east and west." The master of ceremonies then turns to me. "You can see our friend, our brother, our teacher, all the way from the northeast of America.

"The prof is here in more than a dual capacity. He is not coming to witness the bar mitzvah himself [alone]. He is here to represent important dignitaries, like Rabbi Franklin, Rabbi Howard Gorin, and their congregations there in America." I am glad that he then turns attention to "another dignitary with us here at this occasion." It is Dr. Caliben, a surgeon.

"This is a moment of rejoicing, of joy," Emanuel continues. "Our brother is celebrating his bar mitzvah. We thank The

Bar mitzvah kiddush

Almighty for giving us this opportunity. Shalom Yisrael."

"Shalom!" responds the congregation.

"Shalom Yisrael!"

"Shalom!"

Before we leave the synagogue for the outdoor reception, Hezekiah reads aloud the handwritten letter from my rabbi in America:

> Dear Hezekiah,
>
> I wish you Mazel Tov on your becoming a bar mitzvah. Professor William showed me a video of your beautiful leading of services. Please accept this pair of tefillin as a gift on your joyous milestone. I hope that you feel closer to God each time you wear them. I hope we will meet in person someday. Until then, my blessings to you and your family for much joy in your Jewish life.

"Amen," a response rings out. We then exit from the syna-gogue—backwards, facing the Torah left within—to commence the reception. To my surprise, I am handed what looks like a meet-ing agenda. Only then do I realize that, however familiarly Jewish the services portion of the bar mitzvah was, the reception is to be quintessentially Nigerian: protocol will reign, and festivity will be interspersed with formality.

Bar Mitzvah
Chazzan Hezekiah Ben Habakkuk

Reception Programme

1. INTRODUCTION OF THE CHAIRMAN AND MEMBERS OF THE HIGH TABLE
2. ARRIVAL OF THE CELEBRANT
3. OPENING PRAYER
4. OPENING REMARKS BY THE CHAIRMAN
5. PRESENTATION / BREAKING OF KOLA NUTS
6. MUSIC INTERLUDE
7. WELCOME SONG(s) BY THE CHILDREN OF TIKVAT ISRAEL SYNAGOGUE, BYAZHIN-KUBWA, F.C.T. ABUJA
8. MUSIC INTERLUDE
9. CUTTING OF CAKE / DANCE BY THE CELEBRANT
10. REFRESHMENT
11. PRESENTATION OF GIFTS TO THE CELEBRANT
12. SPEECHES BY INDIVIDUAL-GUEST (AS MAY BE DIRECTED BY THE CHAIRMAN)
13. VOTE OF THANKS BY THE CHIEF HOST, ELDER HABAKKUK NWAFOR
14. CHAIRMAN'S CLOSING REMARKS
15. CLOSING PRAYER

We men, and certain women guests, are seated on one side of the courtyard, under an awning. (How absurd to have imagined bringing tarpaulin to Nigeria.) On the other side of the yard, also under a kind of tenting and also on white plastic chairs, sit the other women and young children. We all expectantly await the first public appearance, now that the religious ceremony has been completed, of the first bar mitzvah boy of Kubwa, Abuja, Nigeria. Thanks to the amplifiers hooked up to Habakkuk's private generator (Nigerian electricity supply is notoriously fickle), we wait to the soundtrack of Israeli crooner Boaz Sharadi. As Boaz sings *Etzli hakol beseder* [Hebrew: "Everything is all right with me"], Hezekiah, with just a hint of newfound cockiness in his step, slowly strides across the courtyard, five friends in tow, to take his place of honor next to the High Table. He is wearing a white shirt, light grey tie, dark grey sports jacket, and snazzy black fedora. His friends are also dressed in white shirts and even wider-brimmed black hats. Once Hezekiah and his boys are seated, Boaz Sharadi is muted and Elder Agbai of Gihon synagogue is called upon to pronounce the opening prayer of the reception.

Bar mitzvah boy and friends

Hezekiah and his parents

Bar mitzvah boy's sisters with kid

Next to speak is he who has been introduced at the kiddush as my fellow "dignitary." Dr. Caliben, a full-bearded man with lively eyes and hints of *payess* [Yiddish: sidelocks] peeking from his temples, exudes knowledge, intelligence, and self-confidence. He is originally from Anambra State but lives in Abuja where he has established a clinic that bears his name. He is a medical doctor, a general surgeon, and one of the most recent adult entrants into the Jubo community. As such, from time to time he is called upon to perform as *onye na ibi ugwu*[28]: that is, as *mohel*, or Jewish ritual circumciser. But today his duty is to deliver formal remarks as designated "chairman" of the bar mitzvah reception.

"Thank you, everybody. Special Guest, members of the High Table, Distinguished Ladies and Gentlemen: Let me thank you for honoring this epoch-making occasion. It is one of a kind that has never happened in our midsts, in Abuja. We are so delighted that it happened, and that we are all witnesses to it.

"We wish it will continue. Our faith has come to stay. It goes from strength to strength."

"Amen," someone responds.

"Israel must live!" Dr. Caliben cries out.

"Amen!"

"Igbo must live!"

"Amen!"

"The origins of the Igbo are no more in doubt. We are Israelites, and it needs to be acknowledged by everyone . . . to live by it, without fear or favor.

"When I was in Ireland I was told something that has never left my mind. What was I told? Four things that we must always [remember].

"One is the people. The second is the land. The third is Torah, and the fourth is Hashem. We must always bears this in mind, in every place we are.

"We should understand that we are ambassadors of Israel."

---

[4] In addition to the literal meaning of circumcision, the Igbo word *ugwu* also connotes "perfection" and "respect."

Whatever Jews do as individuals, the surgeon observed, reflects on them collectively. "We must live up to the nationhood that the Almighty has entrusted in us, as a kingdom of priests." As a light unto the world.

"We in Igbo have an adage: 'Someone who is looked up to does not belittle himself.' So we must live up to our expectations. We must set an example, not only to our children, to our children's children, but to others, to emulate. We must live up to what we represent."

The doctor gestures to the other side of the courtyard, where the younger guests are sitting politely. "If you look over there you see children. They are all there. We expect them to grow tomorrow and become leaders. To carry on and to take over from us. It is our duty. Just like our host today has done, taking his son in the right direction. Today we heard the prayer he made. It is still our responsibility to make sure we guide these children up to the age at which they will do their bar or bat mitzvah." Such reference to the coming-of-age ritual for Jewish females—not yet accepted universally within the Orthodox Jewish world—is heartening to hear in Abuja.

"In the same light, I continue to beg for harmony. There is joy in harmony. There is another saying in Igbo, 'When you tie together brooms, you cannot easily break them. But if it is a single broom, you can break it easily.' So we must be united. Go strong, so that we cannot be broken. Only in this unity can we withstand the hostile environment which we are living in. Shalom Israel!"

"Shalom!"

The call and refrain repeat twice before Dr. Caliben concludes with an implicit reference to the Holocaust. (Or is it to the near-genocide of the Igbos during the Biafran War?)

"Israel has come to stay! Never, never, never again. It can never happen again!"

"Amen!"

"There is no going back."

Dr. Caliben recalibrates his tone of voice. "If you look at item five on the agenda," he says, "you will see 'Presentation and Breaking of Kola Nuts.' There is a unique story to the kola nut.

Here in Nigeria, we have three major tribes—Yoruba, Hausa, and Igbo. They say that the Yorubas brought the kola nut. They grow it. They're the ones who plant it. The Hausas they eat it, just like food. But the Igbos *celebrate* it. They make ceremonies with it. They don't just eat it.

"In my studies, I discovered that this kola nut represents what we were doing in Israel." *Lechem* [Hebrew: bread] had been—and in most places remains—the ceremonial food of choice for Jewish blessing. "But when we came here, for one reason or another, over the years we could not continue that very tradition of bread. So instead of breaking bread, we started breaking kola nuts.

"So each time we get a kola nut we must pray. We don't just eat it. It is not just food. We pray before we break it, and share it among ourselves. It represents the [original] breaking of bread.

"In any occasion, if the kola nut is not broken, or presented, to us it is as if the *minhag* [Hebrew: local Jewish custom] has not been [followed]. We also say in Igbo, 'As he is the chief host, he is the one to break it.'" And with that, Dr. Caliben turned the proceedings over to Sar Habakkuk.

Invoking the saying he had shared with me that very morning, Habakkuk explains why he will need to speak in Igbo: "'Kola nut never hear English.' I have to speak in the language that the kola nut will hear [understand]!" Just as Habakkuk raises the kola nut and switches to his native tongue, someone hands me his "mobile." "A student of Rabbi Gorin's wants to speak to you," says the tender of the telephone. "He's in Lagos." As I accept the cell phone greetings of this stranger-brother, Habakkuk continues in Igbo, the only words I catch being "bar mitzvah" and "amen." After the reception, with the kola nut out of earshot, Habakkuk will tell me in English what he said in Igbo:

"I thank God, the Holy One of Israel, who created this beautiful opportunity, this beautiful gathering. I give thanks to Him who granted the journey for my special guests, [you] who traveled all the way from America, and my brothers who came from Ogidi with the Sefer Torah. I give thanks to God for those who are living in Abuja, who came from [the outlying settlements] Gihon, Madala,

Gwari, Dutsi, Suleja, for being merciful with their journey. Because it is not easy to travel. If not by the assistance of Hashem, a step of only one kilometer may encounter destruction. I thank Hashem for bringing them together here.

"I thank my friends, the members of the community and everybody, both Jews and non-Jews. Hashem created this opportunity for *all* of them to be here for the bar mitzvah of my son Hezekiah. May God keep them alive. They left their business, today being Monday—regular business hours—and they leave everything they are doing, their offices, to come here. I bless them thus: Upon whatsoever they put their hand, may Hashem assist them, bless them. May they never lack, for the fact that they sacrificed their time.

"I thank the Holy One of Israel who has blessed me with the opportunity to celebrate my son's bar mitzvah. My father was not able to do it for me, but look—I have the opportunity to do it for my son. I thank Hashem for the opportunity."

Then he prayed for the protection of all Jews and for Israel. "Israel will be like tomorrow—for tomorrow never finishes. Israel will be like a huge palm nut, surrounded by nettles. If you try to cut the palm nut heedlessly, you will cut your hands. Whosoever lands a blow to Israel, his hand will be full of blood.

"Israel is like a rock, a stone. If anyone strikes a knife on the stone, the pieces of the stone will wound him and enter his eyes. He will never see again.

"I blessed our ancestors Abraham, Isaac, and Jacob. We are here today on account of the tradition that they left for us. May they assist us and defend us spiritually, as we are here representing them physically.

"I bless all the women, and bless their children with grace. It is the duty of woman to raise the child. I bless them for raising the children in Jewish culture. . . . A man can have only, at most, six hours a day to stay at home. But a woman has much more time to stay with the child. That is the reason why our Jewish book says, 'Consider a child Jewish if the mother is also Jewish, regardless of the religion of the father.'"

* * *

A show! Jubo girls and boys arrive, dancing in unison across the
Habakkuk compound, singing:

> One step at a time. Only one step at a time.
> This is the way that Hashem will lead you,
> One step at a time . . .

Then they chant in unison:

> "Shalom Israel. We are the kids of Tikvat Yisrael.
> We are here to give you all the best.
> May Hashem bless you all."
> "Amen," we at the High Table respond.

A new melody:

> Welcome, welcome to you all . . .
> Welcome everybody, sitting on the storing chairs.
> Welcome my dear rabbis
> Welcome my dear elders . . .
> Welcome my dear *imas* [[Hebrew: mothers],
>   welcome my dear elders . . .
> Welcome my dear sisters, welcome my dear brethren . . .

One by one, each of the children then approaches the High Table,
addressing the guests. The first one looks like he is six years old.

"Shalom, Israel. My name is Tel Aviv ben Gabriel. I am here to
say the prayer upon waking from bed." He does so in rapid, flawless Hebrew. He steps back, and a girl, only slightly older, takes
his place.

"Shalom, Israel. My name is Deborah Leah. I am here to say
the prayer upon entering the synagogue." She also recites by heart,
in rapid, flawless Hebrew.

A second girl comes forth to say the prayer for forgiveness. A
third girl comes forth to sing a familiar congregational prayer, *Ayn
Keloheinu* ("There is none like our God"). For a change of pace,

another child presents in English:

"Shalom Israel. My name is Tovah. I am here to say the thirteen principles of Jewish faith:

"I believe that God is the Creator. He is sacred. He is incorporeal. He is eternal. He alone must be worshiped. The prophets are true. Moshe was the greatest of all prophets. The eternal Torah was given to Moshe. The Torah is immutable. Hashem knows all our thoughts of mind. In order to punish. The Messiah will come. There will be resurrection. Shalom!"

Each in his or her turn, other children approach and serenade the High Table with other Hebrew songs and prayers. Together they sing *Hu ya'ase shalom aleinu* ("He will bring peace upon us") and then exit, as they entered, dancing, waving their white-gloved hands, and singing the same prayer song to a different melody. This endearing "music interlude" has been wonderfully scripted and choreographed by Hezekiah's mother.[5]

---

[5] True to form as a Jewish mother, Hezekiah's mom will eventually refuse to let me leave for the airport without a dinner container filled with stew and the metal cutlery with which to consume it. (At the security screening, the inspector will admire the liquidy picnic and agree to bend the rules and not confiscate it, inveighing upon me to eat it all up before boarding.)

Friends and entertainers

Bar mitzvah reception tent for younger guests

Dr. Caliben resumes his role as master of ceremonies. "The next item on the list is 'Cutting of cake.'" No sooner is the bar mitzvah cake cut than it is announced that *mincha*—the afternoon prayer—will commence at four o'clock. But there is to be much rejoicing between now and then.

Habakkuk and I enter into a competition: which one of us of us is happier? My claim lies in the success of my voyage and my satisfaction over how well Hezekiah has performed. But Habakkuk wins. "I am happy more than you today because I have the opportunity of celebrating the bar mitzvah of my son. My biological father didn't do it for me. But I am doing it for my son."

Habakkuk later tells me he disagrees with the Igbo saying, "Monkey can't take oath for kid on back." In other words, if Papa Monkey is swinging through the forest, can he know for sure that his child isn't swiping a piece of fruit off of a tree that belongs to another? Could Papa Monkey swear to it?

Rather, Habakkuk subscribes to "A lion's cub never eats grass." He explains: "Our children are our image, our resemblance. If I am bad, they will be bad. If I am good, that's how they will be. My son will behave like me. . . . I am happy to raise a Jewish boy. To bring him along the line of Avraham, Yitzhak, and Yakov."

* * *

The morning after the Big Day, I ask Hezekiah about his future. He is already preoccupied with having to leave home the very next month. He will be going to Lokoja, over one hundred miles away, to become a boarder at the Ozoro Senior Secondary School.

"What do you like to study?" I ask him.

"Science," he replies.

Hezekiah is a serious boy, quiet and respectful. Earlier, he has asked me for permission to go to the synagogue outside of prayer time, just so he could read. When I had asked him what he liked to do for fun, that's also what he replied: reading books, especially about Judaism.

Now I want to know more about his intellectual pursuits. "What kind of science?" I continue. I expect some conventional answer, like biology, earth science, at best something like physics. Instead he throws me for a loop with "Petrochemical."

"Petrochemical," I practically stutter back to the thirteen-year-old. "Why petrochemical?"

"I have small knowledge. I know how to deal with oil."

When I share this conversation later in the day with his father and friend Pinchas, they both join me in laughter. But then Habakkuk turns serious.

"That is why we are crying. After he goes, we won't see him for three months . . . and when they pray in Assembly, in class, it will all be Christian. I would like to meet the principal to plead that Hezekiah be excused from this, and to ask permission for Hezekiah's absence for Jewish holidays."

It will be difficult for Hezekiah, I respond, to be the only Jewish pupil in the school. "To be the only Jew in a school where the others don't know what a Jew is, what Judaism is. They have holidays he won't celebrate. He'll have holidays they won't celebrate. He'll have to make do." But it is the sacrifice he must make, as a Jew, in order to gain the kind of learning that will eventually bring prosperity to his family and to his community.

"We're all going through that," Pinchas soberly adds. "It's not easy."

* * *

Only when I begin to pack do I realize that I have spent the past three days living more Jewishly than I have since summer camp in Israel, more than four decades before. Hezekiah's sister Shalomith "knocking" on the curtain of my room to announce, "Prayer is starting, Sir." The continuous cycle of *tefillot*. Saying grace in Hebrew over every specific type of food (including the kola nut). People routinely lacing their ordinary conversations with *Hashem*, *shalom*, *torah*. Hearing them answer their cell phones with "Shalom!" and referring to each other as "My Teacher." Donning the kippa when entering a home. And even, having overcome my allergy to phylactery and becoming a purveyor of them, joining my hosts in laying tefillin.

I thank Habakkuk and Pinchas for expanding my circle of Jewish community, knowledge, and understanding, for showing me how Igbo contributes to and enriches Judaism. Habakkuk says, "Everyone who supports us spiritually, and otherwise, is encouraging us to keep on. Supporting is not only material things. There is supporting and advice that is greater than material things. I believe that faith comes from hearing. If you don't hear, you won't believe. It is when you hear that you believe."

That night Sar Habakkuk's cell phone rings. It is one of the Ogidi contingent, calling to reassure Habakkuk that they have arrived home safely. "The bar mitzvah is complete," I hear my host say.

He is relieved, but not entirely. It is only three days later, when I phone Habakkuk from America to reassure him that I, too, have returned home safely, that he proclaims—this time with finality—"Now the bar mitzvah is complete."

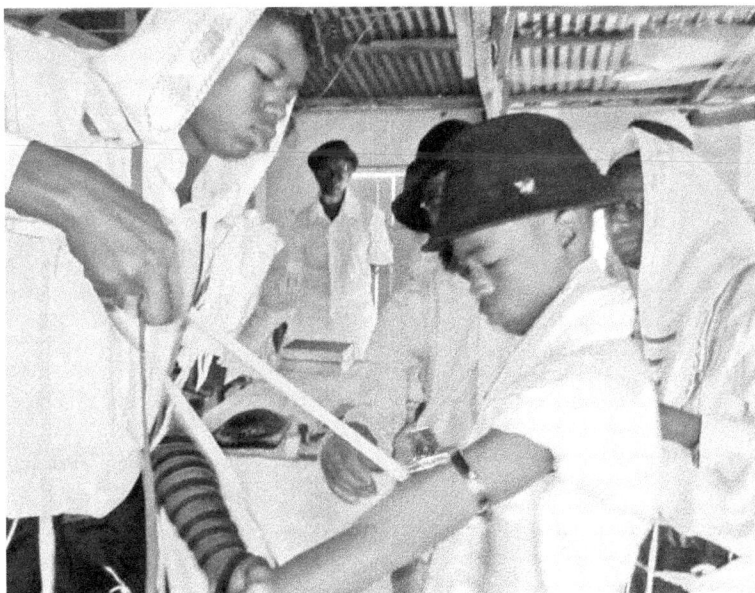

First tefillin binding

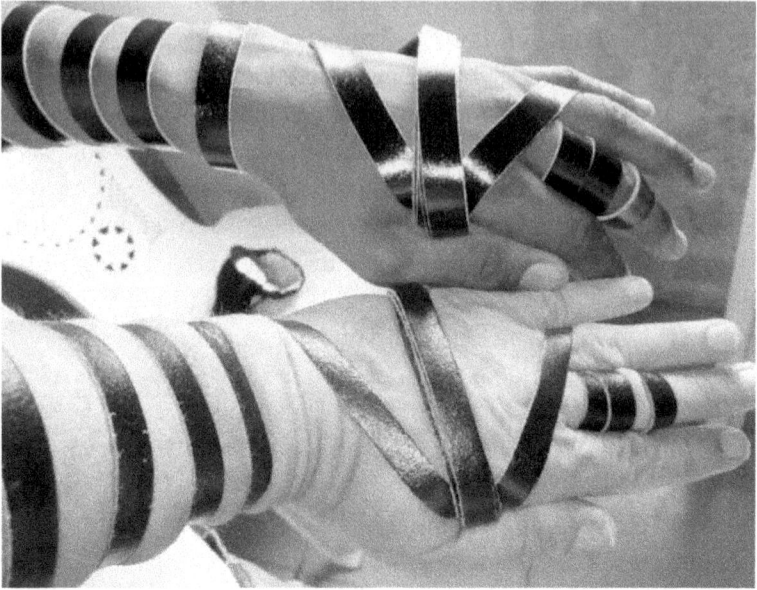

(From top to bottom): Bar mitzvah boy and author

CHAPTER THREE

In Their Own Words:
Jubos Describe
Their Spiritual Journey

"Hashem started us to establish ourselves, and we are working with Him. From here in Nigeria we can help Israel. I don't want to go there and trouble anybody."[1]
—Dr. Lawrence Okah

I was born on November 19 in 1950, in Nsukkah, Enugu State. I read civil engineering at the University of Nigeria and joined the Federal Capital Development Authority as a civil engineer up until 1993. That's when I left the civil service. Now I have changed fields. I have a Ph.D. in theology with emphasis in Jewish studies.

---

[1] As mentioned earlier, this and every succeeding quotation prefacing the Jubo life stories in this chapter are composites of compelling points made by the speakers. The literal phrasings appear in the narration itself.

We started the Jewish movement in 1990. At first there were some Jewish brothers who came down from America to Nigeria, where there were Messianics. I got a pamphlet that was talking about the Holy Name, of Hashem. There were some rabbis listed there, and I wrote to one of them—Rabbi Simcha Pearlmutter—and that's how I became in contact with him. It is he who became my rabbi, who was guiding me when I declared for Orthodox Judaism.[2] He had a community in Israel, Ir Obot. He is late [i.e., deceased] now. They started a small community in Aweri, Imo State, 'til 1991. By 1992 they were to leave Nigeria to settle in Israel. After the Passover, the Pesach, they appointed me the Nigeria leader of the community. They had come specifically for the Igbos. So they handed me over as leader for the revival of the Jewish movement of Igbos of Nigeria.

For Passover 1993, I gathered all of the Messianics together at Oji River, in Rivers State. I told them that the Jewish religion is Orthodox Judaism, not Messianic Judaism. I declared Orthodox Judaism to them. They accepted it, because I was their leader, having [first] received my teaching from Rabbi Pearlmutter, and began to teach the people. That was the first [truly] Hebrew community, in Oji River. We had a minyan there, a standing minyan, and people came there to settle.

Everyone had to copy from my siddur, because that was the only one we had. That was the first thing we had to do. We also got *Teach Yourself Hebrew* and began to copy it. Because our Igbo language is akin to Hebrew, it was easy to learn.

In 1994 there was a problem [in Nigeria], so people started to scatter. I was their leader and so I had to gather my people together. I went to Port Hartcourt, and then to Abuja, where I was planning on how to reorganize the whole people community. First I called it KISON—Kehilla Israel Synagogue of Nigeria. I have not told

---

[2] Note that Dr. Okah is using "Orthodox Judaism" here to distinguish it from "Messianic Judaism," not "Conservative" or "Reform" Judaism. Messianic Judaism incorporates many elements of contemporary Jewish practice while retaining the foundational Christian belief that Jesus is the son of God.

people this, but . . . I was spoken to. I heard a voice saying "KISON is not in the Scripture, not in the Torah." So I asked, "What is the closest thing to KISON?" I was told that the river that left the Garden of Eden and encompasses Kush—which is the Blacks—was named "Gihon." Gihon stands for the lost river of Israel among the Blacks. So instead of KISON I would call it GIHON Hebrew Research Centre. I was hearing these things and they were being discussed in my head.

It was as if an argument was going on in me. For the first time I heard angelic exposition of Torah. They also taught me the Song of the Sea, which I taught to my people. I had never heard the song before. It was just taught to me like that.[3] All the songs the community sings now are those that I would just hear in my dream.

People started coming from other places. Other people. There are more than a hundred synagogues. In Lubweyi and elsewhere, they were Christian Shabbat. I converted them to Orthodox. Here [Abuja], the people are in capable hands. That's why from time to time I go to those places, where they are learning some things [not correctly Jewish] . . .

Israel? I have not gone there. I am not yet connected to the rabbinate or even the embassy. I don't like bothering people. I am just doing what I am doing. We are working with Hashem. He started us. We are going ahead with Him. We are able to establish ourselves. From here we can help Israel. I don't want to go there and trouble anybody. That's why I have not made any attempts to go.

ı

---

[3] In fluent and mellifluous Hebrew, Dr. Okah then sang for over four minutes.

"I always liken my people to that bird that lived for centuries with butterflies and started thinking it is one. But butterfly knows: "No, this is bird!" The best thing is to be ourselves, not assimilate, and live with the truth."

—Dr. Caliben Ikejuku
Okonkwa Michael

I started thinking about my roots, as an Igbo, when I was in India, doing my medical studies. I thought about it for a very long time. In secondary school, in the history books we have in Nigeria, Igbo roots are not described extensively. They summarize in two or three lines. But when they talk about Hausa roots, or the Yoruba roots, it is very elaborate. So I began to wonder: Does it really mean we do not have a root, too? So I started learning about Igbo roots: where do we really come from? Based on research I did abroad, I began to have this inclination that we must have come from Israel. . . . I was not satisfied with Christianity.

In 2007 I had a dream. In that dream somebody told me I should go see someone, a certain man who used to renew my vehicle license. I ignored the dream for thirteen days. Then I had the same revelation—I should go meet that man where he worships. But I did not know where. So I went to where he works and asked, "Where are you worshiping? I would like to go with you." I didn't tell him why.

He said I would not like to go, because it is on a Saturday. I said, "It doesn't matter if it is a Monday, or Tuesday, or Wednesday. I just want to go and see this place."

That Saturday he didn't take me. I went back to him. "Oho, why didn't you call me? You promised you would take me to the place on Saturday." "Okay," he said, "next one." And he took me.

Behold, when I got there, it was a Jewish synagogue, here in Abuja. Gihon. So, I said to myself, "Okay, this is what is happening. After all my studies [into my origins], this is where I have been directed."

I started acquiring more Jewish books. And acquiring more African books, on history. I'm a medical doctor but now I study more history than medical books . . .

Based on what I have seen on the ground, and all the facts, I have come to the conclusion that, actually, we are Israelites. We Igbos, originally, are Jews. We have traced our origins. We have done research. I have studied the Lemba in Zimbabwe. The Jews in India. They look like the people around them. It is God's miracle to make them adapt to their environment so that they can survive. I see it as a survival mechanism.

There is confusion among the Igbos because the white people came and deceived us.[4] Yes, Christian white people. But the reason I first said "white people" is because Israel is in every nation. People always think that Israel has one morphology, or one color, or one tongue. No. Everywhere they sojourn, they look like the people around them. In all the tongues, in all the races, you have Jews. The other day I saw on the Internet some Chinese who made *aliya* to Israel. In Japan, they have Israel. In Middle East, they have Israel. In Africa, they have Israel. But the Gentiles—let me put it that way, because in Nigeria we have Gentiles, too—they deceived us, and we followed their ways. The irony of it is that we can never be them.

I cannot be you. If I want to be you, I can only be a second [a copy] of you. I have to be myself. That's the only way I can make the best out of myself. That's the problem that our people have— they want to be somebody else.

Maybe for now, the bulk of our people are Christians. We don't want to continue living in the error that our parents made. In one hundred and twenty years [since] Christianity has come here, our society has gradually gone down the drain. I have witnessed it going down even in my own life. The things we used to do right, we cannot do them right anymore. Even the elders among us don't even see vices as bad anymore. Our society is tearing apart.

---

[4] At this point, I asked Dr. Caliben to acknowledge—to the mirth of other Jubos in the room—that he must have meant "*Christian* white people." He did so.

One of our earlier authors, called Chinua Achebe, wrote a book, *Things Fall Apart*. That the center cannot hold. At that time we were laughing. We didn't know. But today it's a reality. The center cannot hold. Everybody is just moving from different directions. People don't worship Hashem in the true perspective.

We want to find a way to bring them back, to the system that is ours. I want my people to be themselves, and the only way they can do so is to reclaim their ancestral heritage. That's why we make all the effort to bring them back to the fold.

How? By talking to people. By writing in journals. By importing books.

Which ones? Ah! I have a complete set of *Zohar*.[5] I have Rambam.[6] I have Rashi.[7] I have all the prayer books, Artscroll, Sephardic prayer books. Kai, I have got so many! I have Talmud—seventy-three volumes of the Talmud Bavli [Hebrew: Babylonian Talmud].[8] That one, I bought it for four thousand dollars.

I am very happy. I can even read Hebrew now. The more I study, the more it becomes real to me. So many factors come into play—international politics, international relations. But at the end of the day, Hashem is Hashem. He is unchangeable. Wherever we are, He must seek us out . . .

Anti-Semitism runs deep. It runs beyond physicality. No matter how much Jews try to assimilate, to be part of the [surrounding] people, or to try to hide themselves, they can never completely succeed. Even if you think you are filling your head [with their thoughts], Gentiles will always find out that you are not one of them. Something is in you. Abraham's spark will make them detect you. The spiritual cell in us does not change. That is the cell that the Gentile will always detect.

---

[5] Book of Jewish mysticism.
[6] Maimonides (1135-1204), medieval Judaism's greatest intellect and philosopher.
[7] Medieval Judaism's (1040-1105) greatest teacher.
[8] Of the two versions of the Talmud (Babylonian or Palestinian/Jerusalem), the Babylonian is regarded as the more authoritative. Talmud refers to the codification of Jewish oral law (Mishna) and the exegesis (Gemara) of it.

There is one very small bird in our country here. I always liken my people to that bird. They have lived for a very long time—centuries—with butterflies. Do you know butterflies? They have wings and can fly. That same bird has wings and can fly. At some stage, that bird loses memory and starts thinking it is a butterfly. But if then butterfly sees the bird, he knows, "No, this is a bird!" We may be thinking like them, but they know we are not them. If we try to assimilate, they will ferret us out. The best thing is to be ourselves and to face the truth. It's the only way out.

"In *Pirkei Avot* we are told, 'Where there is no leadership, you should step up to it . . .' So that is how I became the leader of the con-gregation."
—*Elder Agbai aka Ovadiah Avichai*

I don't know the date I was born. At the time I was born there was no birth reg-istry in my area. I was born into a fam-ily of Agbai, Agbai Okeji. I did not know my father; he died before I could know him. I knew my mother. Her name was Ute. Ute Agbai.

I was not baptized. I did not know anything about [Christian] Church. When I was sent to a Methodist Church, they taught us about Christianity. When I finished my secondary school I went to a Catholic college in Enugu, College of Immaculate Conception. I obtained my West Africa School Certificate in Education. After that I worked in a secondary school for a short time, teaching Latin language and mathematics. From there I went to the College of Education, University of Lagos, where I did a Nigerian certificate in Education. Then I went to the University of Ibadan where I stud-ied geology, and received a bachelor's degree. I then did my Niger-ian Youth Service in Kano. From there I got a job to work in Abuja here with the Federal Capital Development Authority. Here I worked until I retired as Assistant Director of Geology in 2006.

With respect to Judaism: all these years, I schooled in the An-glican school, Methodist, then Catholic. They were saying they would not take me since I was not Catholic, but they [eventually] took me. When I came out of university I was attending Methodist Church, where I rose to be an Elder. In 1991 we received some tracts from America, from Cecil Roth, one of the people in the Messianic movement sending teachings from the Bible. My "brother," Yehoshua David, he brought some of the tracts that were sent to one of our brothers here in Abuja. David was then in Deeper Life Church.

The tracts were mostly about the Name. The Name of the Almighty. About Yeshua.[9] About this and that. About proper worship. About Shabbat. After we read the message in one tract, which was about proper worship, I called him and we met in my house. We said, "What do we do now? Because these things that are written here, they cite Scripture but they do not say where to go to follow the path contradicted [in our Church]."

I stopped attending my Church, and Yehoshua David stopped attending his Church. People—including a person next to the Bishop—began looking for me. People in David's church began looking for him.

"Why have you and your wife stopped coming to church?"

I told them, "Well, this is what I have read." I gave them the tracts. "If you can contradict the path stated here, then I will begin to come back to your church again. If not, please leave me alone for the time being."

My wife continued to go to Church for some time. Then I gave her the tracts to read, and she read them. But then she stopped going, after she read the tracts. Then those same people came back to my house, asking me, "You stopped coming to Church but your wife was coming. But now she has stopped. We want to know why." When they asked her, my wife said, "I must be where my husband is." Ho! The same thing happened to this my brother here. Yehoshua David said, "The search is continuous. If tomorrow we come upon a path that contradicts the tracts we hold now, we will go for that one. The search is continuous until we reach the place that Hashem is taking us."

So we started meeting in my house to decide about our next move. "We are not going to Church anymore. What shall we do?" Then there and then we went to meet the person who gave out the tracts. His name is Lawrence Okah.

At that time, he was still attending Church. We suggested to him that we begin meeting together to worship, according to what is shown in these tracts. We finally convinced him and started going

---

[9] The Hebrew name of Jesus.

to his house. He also gathered some other people to worship in his house. But it did not take long before we realized that Messianic [Judaism] was not yet what we were looking for. Because there were so many inconsistencies found in Messianic. We didn't know [what we were looking for] but Hashem was taking us somewhere!

We didn't have any prayer book but we worshiped. We continued like that, keeping the Shabbat. Lawrence learned very fast. He got some other books, and taught us the rudiments about keeping the Shabbat in our homes, in this congregation. We got hold of a siddur, and made photocopies from it. We saw that some of the prayers we were doing in Messianic were not proper. They were calling names that were not needed. They were not part of the Jewish worship.

So when the idea of the Orthodox Judaism came to us, it was very easy for us to accept. Because it allayed so many doubts. So many questions were resolved. Everything was straightforward. Even according to our own local traditions, everything fell in line. Those things from childhood. About the Festival of the New Moon. Circumcision. About the Jewish New Year. Pesach. About the naming of a child, *brit mila*. We had been taught all those things in our tradition. But we did not know that it was returning to Judaism. Only then did those things begin having a meaning to us. Before it was just mere tradition. So we can defend the practice of Judaism even from our own traditions.

From there we started to grow, and began to receive instruction from Abuja and other people. That's how we continued until it reached a point where we said we needed a place to worship instead of staying in his house.

We agreed we would look for a place to worship, instead of staying in Okah's house. Eventually, we were able to secure a classroom in a primary school, at Nyanya, a satellite neighborhood of Abuja.

So we were driving celebrating Kabbalat Shabbat in our houses, and driving to that place on Shabbat mornings to keep the Shabbat for a whole day, until we close.

We continued like that until we had a problem with the school authorities. The school authorities said they were not allowing churches any more use of the classrooms as a place of worship. So there we stopped, went back to [worshiping] in our houses. From time to time we would meet somewhere to hold meetings.

Then sometime, around 1993 or 1994, some Israelis[10] came to Suleja. They were asking whether there was any Hebrew, any Jewish congregations in Nigeria, in Abuja here. They met one of our sisters who was living around that place. Our sister told them that there was a Jewish congregation, that we were meeting before in Nyanya but because of accommodation were not meeting anymore. So they sent a message to her, that she brought to us, to find a place where they could visit us.

So we found a place, a nursery school, where we met upon our invitation. There were five of them that came that day. They came there as we were praying, and they worshiped with us for a period. Two of them began to shed tears. We waited until we concluded our prayer. They told us they were happy to be with us. They encouraged us, and said they never thought they were ever going to see something like this. They would come from time to time.

We hired that place as a place of worship. After some time, the owner, being a Christian, said that he would not continue to allow us to use that place, since we were not calling the name of Jesus. So we left that place. Through some of our elders living around Jikwoyi, we got another house where we started praying. We were still having more and more brothers from Israel, from America, coming to see us there.

We were there when the first Israeli rabbi was sent to Nigeria, and came to us. His name is Oriel—Yisrael Shlomo Oriel.[11] He came from Manchester [Britain, after Israel]. Before he came we

[10] When clarification was obtained, the informant was not sure if they had come from Israel or America.

[11] According to several Internet accounts, Bodol Ngimbus-Ngimbus, aka Rabbi Yisrael Oriel, was born into the Ba-Saa tribe of Cameroon, moved to Israel in 1988, and was ordained by the Sephardic Chief Rabbi who also appointed him rabbi to the Jews of Nigeria. Before moving to the United Kingdom, he had purportedly established Jewish centers of worship and learning in the ultra-Orthodox Mea Shearim neighborhood of Jerusalem. See Wachman (n.d.).

were meeting with other synagogues in Abuja here. There was another synagogue in Lubweyi. Those other synagogues were holding meetings when this rabbi came. He visited us, and those other synagogues, and said that things were not good enough for him to attend the *kedusha* [Hebrew: prayer of sanctification]. So he went to the house of one of our brothers, where he said he could not pray on that day.

After that day we would meeting him in Lubweyi, which he was making as the central place of worship. All of us were going there to worship with him on Shabbat days. During the weekdays he would be in my house, and we would meet him there for shacharit [and other prayers]. We received some teaching from him. After he left Nigeria, the government destroyed the synagogue where he was living, because it wanted to plan [i.e., zone] the area.

Then we made an effort to get a place. Through the help of some of our serious members, we were able to raise the money to build a synagogue in 2005. That is how we have built the synagogue up to the level it is now. That is the progress of Judaism among us here up to this moment. Hashem has been wonderful to us, to help develop some talents in us . . .

After some time, the leader we had been meeting with from the beginning said he wanted to be on his own. He left us, and we did not know what to do. Yehoshua David was still in school at the time. So the synagogue was left under me alone. In *Pirkei Avot* we are told, "Where there is no leadership, you can take up a casual [i.e., temporary] one."[12] So that is how I became the leader of the congregation.

Hashem helped me. Eventually my brother finished his schooling and came back, and he has been very supportive. Hashem

---

[12] *Teachings of the Sages* (literally: *Sayings of the Fathers*) is a collection of ethical maxims of sixty-five Jewish sages who lived from the second century B.C. to the second century A.D. The one to which Elder Agbai is referring in Nigerian idiom seems to be the sixth paragraph of the second chapter: "In a place where there are no men, strive to be [one]." (In context, the word "men" implies individuals who are willing to take charge, show competence, or display valor or righteousness.)

blessed him, so he picked up the Hebrew language quickly. (He was already leading prayers when we were still with that other man.) He has been supporting me in so many ways. He made sure the synagogue would be built. Without him I don't know what I would do. Up until now, he is still one of our *gaba'im*[13] making sure that the services are conducted. He is teaching the Hebrew language to the younger ones.

This he has done without formal training. None of us has had formal training in the Hebrew language. We did it through personal efforts. We just got some books and started reading, trying to get the drift of what we were reading.

Hashem also blessed me in a special way and made it easy for me to learn the Hebrew language very quickly.

That's how it is. That is how Hashem has led us up to this moment.

---

[13] Synagogue facilitators/ushers/beadles/treasurers; singular is *gabbai* (pronounced like rabbi).

"I am not educated. I only went to primary school. But today, because I am a Jew, I can stand before a university graduate and compete with him, without fear or favor."
—Chizoba Ede

I was the second born, in 1972—now a family of eight—in a village called Mgbenu near Agbani in Kano Local Government. I attended community primary school on my farm. I trained to be a mechanic and a driver. I wanted to continue with my trading but I couldn't.

My father is not a Christian. He is a traditionalist. My mother, also. When I grew up I was introduced to the Catholic Church. But I was not a senior member. I stopped going to Church in November 2007.

This, my "brother" Ofobuike, was practicing Judaism back then. We were both living in Abuja at that time but at some distance. When I moved closer to him, I learned the name "Judaism." We would sit and discuss. He would tell me some things and I would reason with him.

I found out that all the things he told me [about Judaism] we used to do, in the village. Everything he used to tell me is in the Bible, that is, the Torah. So we kept on discussing. I told him I would like to follow him to the place where he is used to worshiping. On a Saturday I went with him.

I started practicing Judaism two weeks before Sukkot. Since then, I find out that everything we do in the synagogue, we do naturally, in my home town.

One of the covenants done in our home place, circumcision, the Holy One instructed our grandfather, Abraham. Every male child must be circumcised on the eighth day. It is a must.

The New Moon—we do it, the elders do it. Like my father— any time he sees a New Moon he goes into his room with a kola nut, and then comes out and prays for the blessing of the New Moon. Prays to God in heaven and earth, how Avraham, Yitzhak, and Yakov prayed. He would say, "Father, I call you this time because you have made this moon to be full. So you shall make my blessing full."

For Harvest, Sukkot—we called it the New Year Festival. The elders dedicate the new fruit. That is why I myself found out that I'm in the correct place, where I belong.

I enjoin upon my brothers and sisters to stand upon Judaism. Make sure your children, your daughters and your sons, become Jews. No matter what adversity they might find. I stand the test of time because of my Judaism. My father, my mother, my brothers, my sisters rejected me. But I stand firm because I have found something in Hashem since becoming a Jew.

Progress has started coming. I know what I gained when I was a Gentile. All [wealth] perished. But since I became a Jew, one naira I get, I be glad of it. There is life in Judaism.

I am not educated. I was only a primary school student. But today, I can stand before a university graduate and compete with him, without fear or favor. I could never do this before I was a Jew.

> **"Initially, my wife said, 'No, no, no, I don't want this religion! Because you don't eat this, you don't eat that, you don't do this, you don't do that.' But she saw the change in the way I was living and agreed to join me."**
> **—Israel ben Zohar aka Cyril Okoye**

In Israel, I am known as Israel ben Zohar. Here, the local name is Mr. Cyril Okoye. I was born in the year 1953. I was born a Catholic—my parents were Catholic—and after that entered Christian Fellowship. We used to go to Pentecostal Churches.

In 1991 I came to know about Judaism. It just happened.

One day a friend—by name, Ben Shem Tov—came to us as we were talking and said that he discovered a new thing. We said, "What is it that you discovered?"

"A religion that is our heritage! That religion—its Sabbath is Saturdays." He said we should come to his house.

So we came to his house, brought out our Bible, and were studying the Old Testament. There were so many contradictions between the Old and the New Testament. We were amazed because we [had not even] read it.

We now discovered that our Igbo tradition is so similar to the Jewish way of life. So, based on that we said, "We were in the wrong place. This is where we belong!"

From that time onward we would gather every Saturday to study. When we started, we no longer were praying in the name of Jesus. We were lifting verses from the Old Testament, using our handwriting to write our own prayers, until one day a friend of ours sent a siddur from overseas. From his siddur, we made a photocopy and started praying from it, step by step.

Initially, my wife said, "No, no, no, I don't want this religion! Because you don't eat this, you don't eat that, you don't do this, you don't do that." She said she was used to the old way of life, and she was not going to follow me to do this new thing. It was a family fight.

Over one, two years, she [compared] my old way of life [with] my new way. She saw that there was a change in the way I was living. She then agreed to join me. So all of my children—five boys and three girls—have taken Jewish names. We no longer call them by their local names [but rather] by their Jewish names. Only when we go back to the village are they called by their local names.

In 1993 I had a younger brother—same mother, same father—who was staying in Chicago. I saw the address in the siddur [printed in] New York. I gave him money, and he bought one siddur for me. Some time ago the siddur got lost, in transit, when I was traveling. Just two weeks ago, my sister, who was in Johannesburg, brought me some Jewish books—a new edition of the *Chumash*,[14] *Midrash*,[15] and some other small, small books.

For my family, we are very happy to be Jewish. It is wonderful. For me, it is a religion that is a way of life. But it is very difficult to practice here. By the grace of Hashem we are trying to improve daily.

---

[14] Five Books of Moses (Genesis, Exodus, Leviticus, Numbers, Deuteronomy), which constitute the first five books of the Bible.
[15] Commentaries on and interpretations of the Hebrew scriptures.

"We don't have a rabbi yet, so we went to the village and did our wedding with traditional Igbo wedding rites. Maybe when a rabbi comes, we will have an organized Jewish wedding."

—Eliezer ben David
né Anyim Edward Chukudi

My name is Anyim Edward Chukudi. My Hebrew name is Eliezer ben David. I was born on the thirtieth of November 1976. My native place is in Abia State.

It all began here in Abuja, in the early 1990s. I was in my secondary school, in a family of three. We were worshiping in Lawrence Okah's house, doing it in our rudimentary way. Those who had the financial means were able to photocopy the siddur. I was still in secondary school with no money at all. So I copied the prayers by hand. That's how I started.

In our country's schools you don't find anything about Judaism. In my university days—I read biochemistry at Nnamdi Azikiwe University—I was still able to meander my way and came upon a small [Jewish community] in Oka, Anambra State. So every Shabbat I was with a group, a few other families. There was no structure called "synagogue." Every Saturday someone volunteered his house, which we used as a synagogue.

In 2004 I finished university and came back to Abuja. After moving from one person's house to another, to a primary school—from where we were chased out—we finally came to one completed building here in Jikwoyi, in 2005, 2006. Luckily, we have acquired this land. With our little means, we are able to have this little structure, where no one would think people would be coming to worship the Creator.

From CNN, and other international media, I have seen magnificent synagogues, well- organized Jewish communities around the world. We are still hoping that one day [we will have the same for]

the Almighty, the Infinite, the Holy One of Israel. He has been so generous to us.

Last year, I got married to a "sister" [a Jewish girl]. Some four months back I was blessed with a boy, Eliyahu ben Eliezer, my firstborn. He was circumcised in the synagogue. The Almighty has been very, very great.

We don't have a rabbi yet, so we went to the village and did our wedding with traditional Igbo wedding rites. Maybe when a rabbi comes, we will have an organized Jewish wedding.

"When I was Messianic, I was very zealous to know how our brothers and sisters in the Land of Israel worship Elohim. The year I had this revelation, I embraced Judaism."
—Emanuel Ikegbunam

I was born 4 July in 1963 in Okpaliko village, Idemili North Local Government in Anambra State. I am a civil servant with the local government.

My father is now late Clement Nwoye Ikegbunam. He was in the Roman Catholic Church and I grew up as member of that church, too. I began my journey to [Judaism] as far back as 1977, in Messianic. I embraced [Jewish] Orthodox faith about four years ago.

Before I embraced Orthodox, I had a revelation concerning Judaism which I kept to myself. I only told my wife. But then confirmation of the dream came at the office when, within two weeks, my elder, Paniel ben Yehuda, told me that they had begun worshiping at Igbo Jewish Community Synagogue in Ogidi. I went there and attended one Shabbat service. Since then, I have been a member of the *knesset* [Hebrew: gathering, congregation] to this very day.

By his Infinite Mercy, one of our masters, Ephraim Oba, was the person that the Almighty used to make me the chief chazzan. He is a Jewish leader who has his own knesset—the Association of Jewish Faith in Amawire, Oweri, Imo State. He said he saw the spirit in me.

In Judaism, we are taught that we are students so we learn every day. Through our own personal studies we study Torah and learn Hebrew. In addition to Rabbi Chai ben Dan and Ephraim Oba, there is Chislon Eben. He is another of our teachers, also Igbo, living in Anambra State. Emanuel ben Paniel is taking over from Chislon. We conduct Hebrew lessons in the knesset on Sundays, Mondays, Wednesdays, and Thursdays.

When I was Messianic, I had this feeling that I want to know how our brothers and sisters in the land [Israel] worship the Almighty. I was very zealous to know how Elohim is being worshiped in Yisrael. The year I had this revelation is the year I embraced Orthodox [Judaism].

"There is a problem we are having with the Judaism in Nigeria. Nigerian Jews are always quarreling. We need a teacher to unite us."
         — Emanuel ben Moshe
         aka Emma Shabbath

You know me as Emma Shabbath. I was born in 1931 in Mbanagu Nnewi in Nnewi Local Government Area in Anambra State. My father was named Moses. He was in Anglican Church.

Formerly, I was in CMS, Anglican. Then I left them and joined Christian Shabbat in 1965. I didn't seek [them out]—the Creator called me.

I joined Judaism in 1996. The Creator ordered me to join. In a dream. In the dream he told me about Judaism. To get His people back to him, because they are following other gods. I dreamed that He told me I would be in more trouble if I remained with [the Christian church]. An enemy would pursue me and I would lose my life . . .

People were preparing witchcraft against me. So the Spirit of the Almighty commanded me to go into the bush and fast. I went into the bush—thick bush!—and began fasting and praying. I read Psalms and other books. After five days He called me, to tell me I was a sinner. I began to cry. "You hear My Voice," He said. "Your sins have not finished. But I will save you."

On the sixth day, the Voice came again. A mighty sword from heaven came into my hand! "I give you this power to go and do the work," the Voice said.

"I will go and do the job of Elijah," I replied. After seven days, late in the night, I went back from the bush to my place.

That's what gave me the power to do the work, to subdue the holy enemy, anybody of evil spirit, any false god, every attack. You see, I don't fear any human being.

When I began to pray again, He sent Binah[16] to be my guardian angel. . . . I've moved through Judaism, through people I know. Dr. Ben Shem Tov was my teacher. I took this boy [39-year-old Yehoshua ben Yisrael] as my chazzan.

I don't quarrel, I don't fight. I don't have any enemy around me. They all help me. But there is a problem we are having with the Judaism in Nigeria. A sickness—hatred. No love. Nigerian Jews don't love each other. They are always quarreling. "Talking about nothing."[17] We need help to gather. A teacher to unite us.

I pray for people who are sick. I help them with their problems—financial, spiritual. I worship in Ameka Bet Yisrael [Hebrew: Your People the House of Israel] synagogue, in Anambra State.

---

[16] Binah is the Hebrew word for understanding, comprehension, reason. Emma Shabbath did not elaborate on the name origin or functions of his angel.

[17] That is, gossiping. Without using the Hebrew term, or recognizing its pervasiveness within the universe of congregations, Emma Shabbath also acknowledges in this paragraph the problem of *sinat hinam*—baseless hatred.

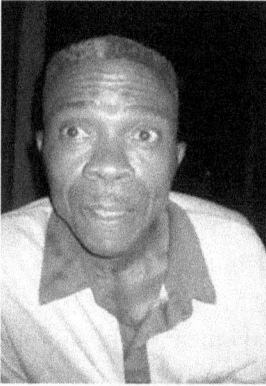

"My wife could not comprehend and insisted that we should go back to Christianity. 'Look,' I said, 'I have found the faith of my forefathers. There just is no going back.' So we parted, just like that, because of the religion."
—Emanuel ben Yonaton né Abor

My name is Emanuel ben Yonatan Abor, from Imo State, eastern Nigeria. I was born the fourth of March, 1958, as a Christian, a Catholic. I married a first wife when I was in Christianity. [But] in 1989, 1990 I discovered the faith, Judaism.

My wife could not comprehend the faith and that led to family problems, a crisis. She insisted that we should later go back to Christianity, and that the marriage would not stand [otherwise].

I said, "Look, I have found the faith of my forefathers. There just is no going back. Either you flow with me, or go your way." So we parted, just like that, [and] had a divorce because of the religion.

After about ten years, in 1998, I married my second wife. Her family, her mother, was already in the faith, through the Messianic branch. But when I married her, she got her family into Orthodox Judaism.

We have four kids now, a boy and three girls. We had two boys, but the second one died. Thirty days ago. He was a bouncing baby boy. But you know, unfortunately, the sad mortality that Nigeria leads to. My children are all with me here [at the synagogue]. My wife, she is not [feeling] fine now, she's in bed. That's why you don't see her.

At the beginning, the community went from a private house in Garki to a private school in Nyanya. Then I returned to Lagos and came back [to Abuja] in 1999. We were going from primary school to primary school, looking for a place. I cannot [deny] that I am the one who found this land [in Jikwoyi], because I'm into property business. I heard that there was this very small land that we could begin to buy and build our own House of Prayer. So that's how we came down here, bought the place, and started—small, small, small, small, until now.

"Because Igbo is from the tribe of Gad, and I am a real Igbo man, I am not a political Jew. I am a biological Jew. "
—Shmuel né Eze Ozoemena

Shalom, Sir. My name is Eze Ozoemena. My Hebrew name is Shmuel. I was born on 28 September 1980, in Ondo State, Ikere, the capital. My family is Christian. They worship in the Ambassador Pentecostal Church. I was following them to the Church.

After I grew up, I went to town and started to go to Assemblies of God. And then, I decided to do a research, on my own, just to know the True God, and how to worship [Him.] I went to a lesson—let me just call it a Kabbalistic lesson. . . . So I found out that Jesus is not the real God. Understand? In the lesson I learned the real God is—let me just call it, in the Holy Tree of Life, Yeheye.[18]

While I was doing this research, this Kaleshi was my friend. We are working in the same area, selling building materials, and he was telling me about Judaism. One day, I just woke up in the morning, came to his shop and told him that I wanted him to lead me to where he is worshiping. Kaleshi says, "Are you ready to go now?"

"Yes, I am ready to go. Come, let us go."

So he leads me to Kubwa, to Tikvat synagogue, where I meet Elder Habakkuk. So I tell him, "I have come here to join you people in worship." He asks, "Are you sure for what you are saying?" I said to myself, "It's okay. Let him begin examining me whether I am serious, or what!"

So I told him, "Yes, I have already made up my mind. Because I am a man for my faith. I have already taken that decision, by myself."

I started going to synagogue, hearing the word of God, searching in the Torah. I discovered many mistakes in the New Testament.

I thank Hashem. I'm a lucky person, the luckiest person in that synagogue—so far [laughs]. Because Hashem said He is going to gather His people in the four corners of the earth. I thank God that

---

[18] Local pronunciation of the tetragrammaton YHWH.

I am one of the Chosen Ones, among those that Hashem has chosen. Because I am a biological Jew. I am not a political Jew. Because Igbo is from the tribe of Gad, I am a biological Jew. And I am a real Igbo man. So I am not a political Jew . . .

What do I mean by "political Jew"? There are some tribes [in Nigeria], like Hausa, sometimes they may practice Judaism. But I am from one of those twelve tribes of Israel. The blood of the Jew flows through my veins.

"After Rabbi Gorin was persuaded to go to my house from the airport, I said to him, 'Don't be afraid. Here is a Jewish home. And it is God Who brought you here.'"
—Sar [Prince] Habakkuk

I was born as a Christian in Abia State, in a town called Mbauchi, in 1957. August 27. I grew up as a Catholic man. I believed in everything I was taught. If I believe in something, I put my head, my eye, my heart, everything into it to follow. Abia is where I married.

It was the week of my marriage, in 1990, when I was called spiritually. In a dream a prophet came to me and gave me this prophesy—that Catholic is not my portion, that I am not called to be there. I went to the elders and asked them the meaning. They told me that I had a call, that the way of Christianity is not my way, that going there is a waste of time. That I must come out of Christianity.[19]

My wife, in our language, is named Amaka Wafu. [She also has a Hebrew name]. I told her, "My wife, my call is not there, in the Catholic."

I thank God for giving me a wife like that, who listens to me, who obeys me, and who takes my instruction. Because whatever I say—that is how we are going to do it. She will not argue. She will follow me.[20]

I had my first issue [child], a daughter, Odoka, at the end of 1991. After that my wife agreed with me, that we become Sabbatarians, Christian Shabbat.

We call it "Christian Shabbat" because [its followers] still be-

[19] For a more detailed version of Habakkuk's spiritual journey towards Judaism, one emphasizing the prophetic, see chapter four, "Tour of a Jubo Shrine."
[20] But see how in chapter four Habakkuk consults with his wife and depends on her judgment about the most critical decisions in their lives.

lieve in Jesus Christ. They still pray in the name of Jesus. Those
who know the Hebrew name still pray in the name of Yehoshua
ha-Mashiach.[21]

After a time—I think in 2002, ending—a "brother," named
Keesh, had a problem. He was working with an engineering company and somebody laid a false allegation to sack him. The company agreed. I said, "Let me see what I can do."

So I did the prayers. I came back and said, "What that man plans
to do to you is what is going to happen to him. And the company
will take you again." [This is what happened.] Keesh came back,
gave thanksgiving, and said, "Well done!" Then he preached to
me. About Judaism. Yes, Keesh, he's the one that told me!

He said, "Father— you are like my Father, so I call you that—
I want to tell you something. Bring me your Torah."

"I have Bible, but not Torah," I told him.

"So bring me your Bible." He started showing me so many mistakes in the New Testament which even I, though his "father," did
not know. Too many mistakes in the New Testament. Falsehood.
Contradictions. I just didn't know it. That is just where we were
before [spiritually].

After this, I take my research. And I said, "Yes, Keesh gave me
very good news." I began to practice Judaism.

I was practicing for one year, but I didn't know my left and my
right. Except that I knew that I didn't believe any more in Jesus. I
believed in the Holy God, the God of Abraham, Isaac, and Jacob.
That was how I was practicing my own Judaism back then. I didn't
even know the prayer for after washing hands. That is what I was
doing until the first coming of Rabbi Gorin.

How I first got to know him was a miracle. It is God, the Holy
One of Israel, who brought Rabbi Gorin to me. I hadn't known
of the rabbi, and the rabbi didn't know of me. I never sent him
an invitation. His intention was to see another person in Abuja.[22]

---

[21] Hebrew: Joshua the Messiah. Yeshu (Jesus) is the diminutive of Yehoshua.
[22] On account of the delicate nature of the episode and the sensitivities of the
various people concerned, I will refer to this person merely as "R."

This is how it happened:

Somebody in Port Harcourt informed my brother that a rabbi was coming to Abuja. What do we do? And I thought, "A rabbi must be my friend." I went into my chamber, my shrine, and prayed. I said, "God: This rabbi that is coming—if You are the one who sent him for Your Lost Tribe of Israel, allow him to come to me so that he will not be cheated or led astray. Do not allow him to enter into bad hands. But if he is not the right man, allow me not to see him." Then I came out of the shrine.[23]

Nigeria is too critical[24] and very dangerous. Too much for one man. We started arranging things for Rabbi Gorin's arrival but had no way to contact him. I sent my friend Yermiahu[25] to go to the airport to wait, to see whether Rabbi Gorin is really coming or not.

Rabbi Gorin arrived at the airport and came out asking for R., the man he was supposed to meet. But R. had disappeared. Do you know why?

R. only knew Gihon [the other synagogue in Abuja]. He told the synagogue people there that a rabbi was coming. A Conservative rabbi. And they said they don't want a Conservative rabbi. Because they are Orthodox. Now, R. had claimed to be the "owner" of Gihon, and didn't know where else he could bring Rabbi Gorin. He didn't know there was anybody like Habakkuk. So the rabbi was stranded.

Yermiahu, the friend who I sent, went up to him and said, "Are you Rabbi Gorin? I was sent by Habakkuk to come and welcome you."

"Yes," he said, "but I am looking for R. I want to see R." But they couldn't get R. on the line. He had switched off his phone. They tried for thirty minutes, for an hour. It was getting late!

Finally, Yermiahu said, "Come. Habakkuk is at home, waiting for you."

"Habakkuk? Is he a Jew?"

---

[23] See chapter four for a "tour" of Habakkuk's shrine.
[24] That is, full of crises.
[25] Jeremiah.

[Yermiahu eventually persuaded the American rabbi to accompany him out of the airport. The sun was beginning to set. They drove to Habakkuk's home in the Jikwoyi neighborhood of Abuja. But the rabbi, justifiably suspicious, apparently refused to proceed further without seeing or speaking with R., the only contact he had been given in Abuja. Habakkuk takes up the story again.]

We started calling R. again. For another hour we still couldn't get him.

"Rabbi Gorin," I said, "don't be afraid. Here is a Jewish home. And it is God who brought you here. If not for the power of God, you would not be here, because I prayed before you came. And the way I am very close to God, if you are not for us, you wouldn't be here. But you *are* here. This is your home."

[The future Chief Rabbi of Nigeria stayed with Habakkuk—despite the latter's modest means and social station—for four days. According to Habakkuk, wealthier people than he in Nigeria could more easily have gained access to Rabbi Gorin. He resumes:]

People with power would have pushed me out. But the Holy One of Israel decided, "Go to Abuja, and seek my servant Habakkuk." Gorin's intention was to come and see R. If he had, I would not have met him. Gorin did not know that it was God's intention for him to seek Habakkuk. . . .

I took him around, to other synagogues, until he traveled to the East and returned to America. For he felt tired. Very tired! After that he sent us materials. He sent computers, saying he would set up a cyber café. They are there, still in boxes, and we are waiting for his command. . . .

In our synagogue we read Torah,[26] siddurim and practice circumcision of newborns. Even in Igboland, we used to practice the festivals. Except for Pesach. Sukkot, in my tribe, we call Afialou. Shavuot is Ufe Gioko. And New Moon is Omwofo.

Pesach [Passover] we took on from when we were in the Sabbatarian Church. But we would practice as in ancient time, as in

---

[26] In the absence of a scroll, Torah readings are conducted from the *Chumash*, the Five Books of Moses in a bound and published version.

the Old Testament. We would slaughter a ram, roast it, keep it clean, and eat it without breaking the bone, as it said in Scripture. And we would march out from the synagogue, and go around, as if we were going out from Mitzraim [Hebrew: Egypt] and come home late at night. That is how we would do it then.

But now that we are in Judaism, we do not do it that way anymore. Because no more Temple. No more roasting of ram. And no more walking out from the synagogue and going out in the street. We have stopped that very one. Now we practice it as our masters teach us. With the Seder plate. All the symbolic food is here, including the leaves, the carrots. . . .

Rabbi Gorin sends documents to us. He sent prayer books, and we do as it is written. We have Haggada,[27] we recite the prayers. When it is time for four questions, the children do it. Drinking of the four cups of wine. . . . I can sing for two hours at the Seder, in English, Igbo and Hebrew.

---

[27] Guidebook for the Passover Seder (home service and ceremonial meal).

"It got into my dreams. Even when I was sleeping I had thoughts about how Christians came to Nigeria. Along the line I saw truth about the True God of Israel."

—Kaleshi Oku

My name is Kaleshi Oku. I was born in 1978. My family was Christian. I finished my secondary school in 1993. At that time I was a member of Christian Kingdom, following my family, my father attending church. But my spirit told me that the tradition was not up to that of Greek people.[28]

In the year 2003 I went to Abuja to do business with my brother. I began searching to know the true God. There I learned that the system of worship was already in our Igbo culture.

The one who first brought me to know Shabbat was Elder Habakkuk in Abuja, whom I did not know in the east. I was not well, I had a problem, and somebody referred me to Habakkuk, who cured me. With herbs.

He began teaching me how to know the true God. I was so surprised to learn that Israel people were not worshiping as like Christian people. I was asking him, "Why is it that Israel are not worshiping like Greek people are used to worshiping?" He said that Israel tradition is like Igbo tradition. "Give me some reasons that will make me sure of what you are saying," I said. So he told me that when a child is born in Igboland, at eight days, he will have a circumcision. I searched, and saw that it was true. And also about the system of kosher. He spoke about ancient people in the Bible. He told me that all the prophets who spoke in olden time were Israel people—all those prophets, Jeremiah, Moshe, Isaiah, were Israel people. He asked me, "In all the churches in Nigeria, have you ever seen a Greek man be a prophet that the world knows?" I said, "No, I haven't."

It got into my dreams. I began searching. Even when I was

---

[28] Greek is used here to mean "gentile."

sleeping I had thoughts about how Christians came to Nigeria. I was so surprised. And along the line I saw that there was an element of truth of what Habakkuk was saying about knowing the True God.

When I looked around I saw that there was no place in the Bible that Greek people were known, where they were the people that God taught to teach others how to know Him.

I asked him, "Why is it that the [Christian] Churches are known in Nigeria, but Israel people are not coming to Nigeria to tell Igbo people how to know the true God? They are the ones who are supposed to come. Why are the Israel people not coming?" He said that I was supposed to ask myself.

So I began searching, thinking, how does this happen? Even in many churches you won't see an Israel man saying he is the one that God ordained to teach people to know Him, to worship, to direct God. There is nowhere in Igboland where you will find him. No, no, no you will only see a Greek or Roman.

So that took me in a direction, and I was wondering, searching. Eventually I saw that what the Christians taught us was a fallacy, a lie. So I followed the way of Elder Habakkuk. I followed him to know it was true. I was so grateful, so happy. God who made me to know Elder Habakkuk. I ask Him to give Habakkuk long life. To secure His people in this evil country. This is our country. It is an evil country. God will help him. Shalom.

"The same Hebrew I was studying while awake, I would dream I was learning in a class, writing it on a blackboard. When I would wake up, I would memorize it all. It became easier to learn."
          —Cantor Moshe né Iheanacho
          [Igbo: "What Was Looked For"]

I was born in 1980 in Kano, in a mission, on 25 December. I grew up in what I call a "Jewish spirit" home. I even used to call it a "Jewish-Christian" home. The reason is, I was born into a family that observed Shabbat, Christian Shabbat. I didn't know anything about Sunday worship, or anything like that.

My mother had problems having a male child. She had had girls, girls. So, on the sixth of Passover she went to the Feast and there—as the doctrine was—a man, a prophet, told her that God would bless her with a male child: "Don't weep again. By this time next year you will have a male child. Your husband, your family, quarreling, wanting to chase you out of your husband's house because of no male child—this will end. God will give you a male child. Call him Moses."

At full time I was born. I was the fourth-born. So my original name was Moses. But my mother also called me Iheanacho, an Igbo name, meaning "What Was Looked For."

I had my primary school in Kano. I started my secondary school in Port Harcourt, and finished up in Abuja. Government Secondary School, Garke Area 10.

I then decided to look for work because I could not afford more schooling then. I sat for the National Examination Council in 2005, 2006. Then I got employment at the National Library and worked there for five years as a library assistant.

After that the government retired our group, so I had no choice but to self-employ.

I was told how Shabbat was erected in Igboland, at the mission [where I am from]. There weren't any missionaries from abroad. We were told that in River State there was a man, a village prophet, named Elijah Bakana. He was preaching, calling people together for prayers on certain days, telling them how to go to church, bringing them to the word of God. He had the power of curing leprosy, the paramount disease at that time. We were told then that people were punished with leprosy. They would come to him to cure them. In curing, they would now know Shabbat [through Elijah]. And that's how the Igbos began to keep Shabbat, according to what we were taught.

The grandson of this Elijah Bakana was Ode-Kete. He went and settled in Awkete and had more disciples. My parents found Ndubi, where they attended festivals. We used to go for three annual festivals, as in going to Jerusalem, to celebrate Passover, and Tabernacles, and the Feast of First Fruits. So all the rules in the Torah, like *amida* [Hebrew: the "standing" prayer], *kashrut* [Hebrew: the laws of keeping kosher]—all these things were practiced, observed, in the next mission. So there I knew more about Old Testament law than about the New Testament. I saw Hebrew letters in the Bible.

When I grew up, I began to read certain things. Then I came across some friends who introduced me to Internet, browsing. I didn't know anything about Internet before. I found Hebrew. Psalm 119. I took my time to copy it out. Twenty-two letters.

From this level now of Sabbath-keeping, we ascended to Messianic. In the Messianic, I got the address of Mister Aharon Chamberlain, and began to write him. He sent me pamphlets about the same Shabbat, the same festivals, and their Hebrew names. But all in Messianic. Gradually, we began practicing Messianic. Although on the Sabbath, we practiced everything we see in the Scripture, like sacrifice. Getting rams and slaughtering them. But this is not in Messianic. So Messianic stopped us from such practice. . . . At this point we were vocalizing the four Hebrew letters of God.

Now there was a brother, from the same Sabbath that I was born. His name was Elijah Elijah. He traveled to Israel and changed his name to Eliyahu Eliyahu. The first time he came to our Church he

was Messianic. That was first day I saw tallit. We were a little confused because of our zeal to know these things, but we didn't have
the access of getting them. We even went so far as to have these
Islamic *tazbi*[29] as part of our practice. We were using it in our
church with incantations, as were taught then.

When [Elijah] came, he said, "This is not, 'Bind them as a sign
upon the arm.' It's a different thing." He began to tell us about
tefillin.

So he then traveled and came back after some months. He was
putting on black suit, black hat, and some white ropes coming out
of his clothes. We now asked him, "What is this?" And he said,
"We have to wear this garment, according to the Torah, as a sign
to remind us of the law of Hashem when we want to go astray. It's
called *tsitsit* [Hebrew: ritual fringes]." So then we know what it is.

We used to enter our church with empty toes.[30] We would wash
our hands, wash our feet, just like our brother Muslims do it. When
Elijah Elijah came, he said, "No, Jews don't wash toes. Wear shoes.
Wash your hands, but not your feet." So we begin to amend.

He brought a siddur, and showed it to us. But I still believed in
this Yeshua [Jesus]. So I took my time to open the siddur from
verse to chapter, from page to page, looking for Yeshua. But I
didn't see Yeshua. I saw the Hebrew, and I saw the English. I was
looking on the English side to see the translation. But I didn't see
[the name]. So I decided there was no Yeshua. . . . The Jews don't
believe in Yeshua. But why are all those Americans telling us about
Yeshua?! Chamberlain was still writing to me every day, about
Yeshua. . . .

One other brother got me a pamphlet telling me that the verse
in Isaiah chapter seven, verse fourteen, was a mistranslation. It said
people purposely translated it that way to suit the New Testament.
The original text said "woman with child." But the Christian Bible
said "The virgin." I doubted it. "I said, 'No, the pamphlet isn't
true.'" I even quoted Chamberlain. We were still in Messianic [but]

---

[29] A kind of rosary, used for counting blessings.
[30] That is, barefoot.

with doubting spirit, still looking. "Are we sure, are we sure?" We weren't very sure.

Then Eliyahu Eliyahu brought the Tanach, for the first time. He showed me. I didn't see "virgin." But there was "virgin" in my Bible. I begin to think, and had second thoughts. This thing is true, what our friend said. I concluded that, yes, the New Testament is not Jewish. But we did not yet have zeal to go into Orthodox [Jewish] faith.

I began to make research, I began to ask questions, through Internet, asking some rabbis. I went to Jewish chat room. I asked questions. They answered. Their answers sounded so Jewish, so different.

I told my Dad, "We cannot continue with this Messianic [Judaism]. We have to change to Orthodox." He said, "My son, anything you say, we do."

[But] my brother-in-law was a pastor in the Church, in the Sabbath Church. He didn't want to change. He was delaying. He was delaying. "We have to have a prophesy, to see a vision, healing." They tell you to bring money, that they will call you, still preaching. So he was in that same [Messianic] Sabbath line. He didn't want to change.

But I went to him, discussed with him, and told him, "This is the fact. The Tanach is Jewish. But your Bible is English. The Hebrew is the original. So why not follow the original?" He kept on turning, procrastinating. Finally, he just left for Lagos, and abandoned the church. So I had to take over, as the leader. But I had friends, with whom I worship, so we were together.

I began to chant, in English at first. In my family we all have that gift—we all sing, we sing well. Gradually, gradually, we were learning together, praying together, in English language.

Then I met my elder, Elder Azuka [Pinchas]. He gave me a siddur. It was Messianic, but it had transliteration. So it was good help to me. Through the transliteration, I could now understand what the characters were talking about. That is how I began to learn to chant in Hebrew.

Even in my office, I was called "the Jew," 'cause I wore kippa, wore it everywhere. I was so serious. I wear black and white. I want to be Orthodox. I want to be Orthodox. I want to learn how to read Hebrew fast!

Hashem saw my zeal, and really encouraged me. When I would wake up at the midnight to pray, with a dictionary, I would pronounce words in Hebrew, and see somebody come to me in the back and say, "No, you don't pronounce it this way, you pronounce it that way." In my head, I would hear a voice [correcting me].

Even in my dream, I would be attending a class. The same Hebrew I was studying [while awake], I would dream I was learning it in a class. Somebody was writing on the board, teaching me Hebrew in the dream. When I would wake up, I would memorize the whole thing. It became easier [on account of the teaching in the dream].

One day I decided to go to RCC [the Israeli construction company operating in Nigeria], to see if I could discuss with a white Jew. I went there and I met Zack Ashkenazi. He saw my kippa, and I told him I was a Jew. He said, "You're a Jew? That's fine. Baruch Hashem. What's your name?" I told him.

"Moshe? Sit down." But he was doubting me, really doubting me. He was still looking at me and was frightened. They didn't want to open up to me.

I told them, "I am Jewish. I want to learn Hebrew from you. In fact, I want to hear you read the hard sounds."

When he saw me with the Hebrew letters, and the photocopies, he asked, "How did you get this?" I said, "From Internet, from friends. My friend who came from Israel, he brought me siddur and I made photocopy. Can you read it? I want to hear the sounds. I want to hear it."

He said, "I don't have a cap here. Can you help me with your own cap [kippa]?" Then he read. And they began to open up. He introduced me to someone else in the compound, Shmuel Assaf. That was at a holiday period. So for the first time I saw Hanukka candles, and they gave me some, to celebrate Hanukka. They told me he would help me read the Hebrew, but I should continue to study.

They promised they would come to the synagogue and see how we are doing. They were promising, they were promising. But they never came, not for one day. Eventually, the synagogue was demolished.

So from there, I began how to learn to read Hebrew, gradually. I learned to lead services in Hebrew, although it would take more time. A service that was supposed to take three hours, we would take six hours, or seven hours. So the service was getting boring. The congregation was not happy. Some of them said, "You should understand the language you are using. Use English." So I used English. I used Hebrew, I used English. Gradually, gradually . . .

Then, in 2004, we had a visitor. It was the first time I saw a rabbi. It was Rabbi Gorin. He came to our synagogue. He saw what we were doing. He saw our siddur. He saw our efforts. He gave me a shofar. Even from my childhood, I know to play trumpet. I'm skilled with all those [musical] things—singing, blowing trumpet, and drums.

After a year or two years, Rabbi Oriel came, an Orthodox rabbi. He saw my efforts. He saw my interest in the faith. He gave me a book, *How to Teach Yourself Hebrew*, and mandated me to teach Hebrew. But I wonder. I had not even prayed with him, for him to hear my prayer and to know how fluent I was in my Hebrew. I don't know who told him to get the book that he gave me. From that day I started to teach the kids. . . .

Before, my synagogue and Gihon used to have combined services. During festivals, Gihon worshipers would come to our synagogue, and I would come to their synagogue. Every time I came, the elders there allowed me to pray.

When my synagogue was demolished, I had no choice. I decided to locate to Jikwoyi, to the Gihon synagogue. That's how I became their leader. I joined the leaders, who were saying the prayers, as one of the prayer leaders there.

"It's not because of my wisdom I decided to join the religion. Only the Holy One of Israel knows why He chose me."

—Nnambe Ibe

I am from east—Imo State. My own town is Obodoukwu. I am from a family of four—three boys and one girl. I was born in 1980, August 31. My father died when I was seven years old. I am single.

After finishing Obodoukwu primary school I went to Kwara State to start junior secondary school with my half-brother. After six years I came back to my own town, and then to Abuja, to serve one of our village men. I stayed with him for four years, and then became master of my own self.

One of my village brothers told me about Judaism. We discussed some things, and I saw that all he told me was the truth. I've accepted and joined to be one of the members of Judaism.

Since then, I've seen changes in my life, in my business. I've decided this is my inheritance. Sometimes I go back home. They—even my mother—ask me, "What do you see, being a Jew?" I told her, "It's not because of my wisdom I decided to join the religion. Only the Holy One of Israel knows why He chose me."

"Because I have been practicing Judaism, my wife has decided to abandon me with my two kids. If that should be the case, she should leave me like that. My children will know the Truth."

—Ofobuike Ani

I was born in 1971, in Mbogodo do Enugu State, into a family of six. I am the last born, and the only boy of the family to have left the village.

My parents are traditional. In my village there is a big "cathedral," [but] I haven't gone into that church since I was born. Not even one day. Up to this date, I decided not to go in there.

After some years I left my home town for Abuja, for work. (I am a driver by profession.) There was a church that I was attending. [On account of] a problem I had with the church I stopped going. [Here is what happened:]

When I had my second daughter, I brought her to another church to be named. The owner [sic] of the church I usually attend was annoyed with me. He told me, "Since you decided to take your daughter to another church to be named, you cannot participate in the activities of our church. But in terms of donating money, you are free to donate money." I thought, "What is the need?" So I decided to [leave]. Every Sunday I would stay in my home.

Shortly after, I met a man called Daniel, a former student of Habakkuk. He told me about this Judaism. Almost eighty-five percent of what he was telling me about Judaism is what I had been doing at home with my father. The God Who made heaven and earth showed me the way. Because if that other man had not stopped me in his church, his "business center," I don't think I would have had the chance to meet this man, Daniel. That is where my practice of Judaism started. The Holy One of Israel made me see the way.

I have been practicing Judaism for six years now. Even as I am sitting here talking to you, my wife has decided to abandon me with my two kids. If that should be the case, she should leave me like that. My children will know the Truth. If the Lord of Israel can give me the strength to bear this, I will come through this strongly.

My wife, and some of my family, decided to reject me. All I have lost is in the past. I am alone, with my kids, but not under any man or woman control. My name is Ofobuike Ani.

"When I read Deuteronomy 6:4, it says there is only one God. There is nothing [to] Jesus Christ being our savior. Only God will be our savior. Messiah—Moshiach—has not yet come but will. There is no one else who has already come."

—Paniel ben Yehuda

Paniel ben Yehuda and wife Lizben Agha

My name is Paniel ben Yehuda from Nimo Mjikoka Local Government. My father is Yehuda. He was not a Jew, but I gave him a Jewish name before he left.[31] He accepted it. He was a Christian. I was born in 1957. My wife's name is Lizben.

Before becoming Jewish we practiced what we called "Christian Shabbat." I became a Jew in 2006, when Rabbi Chai ben Dan came from Israel. He is an Igbo man living in Israel, for something like eighteen to twenty years. He became a Jew in Israel. We met at Oba in Anambra State. He told us about this faith, Jewish faith, at our church. He said that it is of no use to practice Christian Shabbat. Rather [it would be better] to practice Jewish faith. That is what our people in Israel [are] practicing. He is the one who told us there is nothing [to] Jesus Christ being our savior. Only God will be our savior. I believed him, because when I read Deuteronomy 6:4, it says there is only one God. There is no one else who has already come. He is the one who said that Messiah—Moshiach—has not yet come but will. He is the first person who taught us about Torah, not Christian Bible. And to tell us about Hebrew. Since that time we communicate with him, by phone or Internet. My wife agreed with me, because she liked the truth.

In 2008, Rabbi Gorin came to our Knesset in Ogidi. He brought us so many books—*Chumash*[32] and Etz Hayim.[33] With my son,

---

[31] That is, passed away.

[32] The Five Books of Moses in bound book form.

[33] *Chumash* of the Conservative Movement of Judaism.

Emanuel, I have been studying Hebrew. Elohim of Israel has given him the talent to teach us. Our synagogue is Igbo Jewish Community Synagogue in Ogidi, where I am an elder, looking after the synagogue. The gabbai is Yehuda ben Moshe, and the chazzan is Emanuel Ikegbunam.

"Some months ago I had the opportunity of bringing my children—my two sons and my daughters—to the synagogue, for the first time. They all followed me to the synagogue. What joy!"
—Pinchas né Prince Azuka

In August 1956 I was born Azuka Ogbuka'a. (Actually, it is Ogbukaya but Ogbuka'a is the abbreviation.) I was born in Abala-Ona in Ndokwa East Local Government of Delta State, from a royal family. A traditional Christian family. Presently, my father, Frederick Ogbuka'a, is the Obi, the traditional ruler, of the Abala kingdom. He is a retired education inspector. At the secondary level I had professional training in marketing. I will leave the rest and go straight to how I found myself into [Judaism].

As a Christian family, my father had traveled plenty—been to the United States, to Britain, where he actually had his educations and training. At a point in time, I had these questions for him:

"We are Christians. Why is it most Jews I have read are not Christian? And the center of our worship, Christ, was a Jew. Yet they are not Christians." (Incidentally, he told me that he himself has questioned—that what I said was true, but that he had no answer for me. So we stopped there.)

At another occasion I asked him, "You circumcised me."

"Yes."

"Why?"

"Because it is my father's tradition. Our fathers' tradition."

"At what date did you circumcise me?"

"On the eighth day of your birth. That's our tradition."

"Are you circumcised yourself?"

"Yes."

"Then why?"

At first he didn't answer. Then he said, "It is our fathers' tradition, our culture." We stopped there.

We also have this traditional New Moon celebration. It's like a feast. Every moon. He said, "That's how we make it. To celebrate the New Moon." But he didn't give me any reference to the Jewish people. He did not.

I continued in my Christianity but started raising personal questions. By 1998 I had left the Anglicans for Born Again. Because I want to go to heaven.

One of the basic questions I asked was, "Yes, we are Christians. But Christian Sabbath is Sunday. Who changed it? And why? On whose authority was it changed? And where was it changed?" Unfortunately, we had not access to books. The answer always was, "You can't get all the answers [to your questions now] until you get to heaven."

I was not very comfortable with that answer. All the same, I played along. I played along. But at a point, it became difficult for me.

I discovered Seventh Day Adventist, where I was given books. One in particular was *The Great Controversy*. I had this urge to keep the Commandment as instructed. And I decided to begin keeping Shabbat—on my own, because where I was living there [were] no other Adventists.

In 2000 somebody gave me a pamphlet, a tract, written by Aharon Chamberlain from the United States. That's when I began the teaching from the Messianic organization.

I wrote and was sent another Messianic document, a book, *Torah Rediscovered*. I started feeling uncomfortable. I said, "No." I started keeping Shabbat in my own house. In a total disagreement with my wife! We are quite opposite. I left where we were living together and moved into the city.

At that point in time, I couldn't hold it anymore. I begin to search in a state of confusion. Until 2001.

I met a gentleman. We were worshiping together in my house. He said, "What are we doing in Messianic? It is not the whole thing. We still have to continue." That was how I was introduced to Gihon. With all the doubts. With all the doubts. How to deny the other center of worship. It was a problem to me.

Yet I got a certain conviction! Because there, in Gihon, I was taught the shema. Because Ovadiah Avichai—Agbai—told me, "When you recite shema, you are actually saying, 'It is Hashem and Hashem alone.'"

He stopped me there and taught me the difference between monotheism and polytheism. "Monotheistic faith is the belief in one God, and that God becomes your God. Your Savior, your Redeemer, Your Deliverer. And all in all. You cannot believe in that One and only God, and at that same time also believe in another Savior. And that is the center of Jewish worship, monotheism. One God.

From that time on, until this time, I have not been going back, I have not looked back. I've begun to see. As I study Torah, I begin to see the relationship between certain things we practice in our traditional culture that almost tally with the Torah. Circumcision I have mentioned earlier. New Moon, and a very strong teaching we have between offspring and elders—respect for elders. In sharing, in sharing communal life. After harvesting, leaving part of our farm, the corners of our farms for the less privileged. We still do this up until this day. Great attention and care for the widow and the orphan. As I began to study, and to learn, I discovered that these things [Igbo practice and Jewish teachings] are intertwined. . . . Within the last year, Gihon has celebrated its first two bar mitzvahs. . . .

I personally have been so enriched with the help of people like Rabbi Howard Gorin and Rabbi Oriel ben Shlomo, and so many others. Not just I, but so many of us! So many people that the Almighty has used to bless us. . . .

Disagreement is still there with my wife. We are still living separately, as a result of this. Other members of my family do not fully accept what I am doing. My father is liberal about it. He is not complaining. My mother, too, is liberal about it. They don't stop me.

Some months ago—my wife recently agreed—I had the first opportunity of bringing all my children to the synagogue, for the first time. They all followed me to the synagogue. What joy! My two sons, all of my daughters who were around then. Even my first daughter has no problem with it. She is comfortable with it.

My first two kids are girls. Blessing, the first, is married. Chidima—meaning "Hashem is good"—is nineteen and is graduating from university next year. My first son, Joshua, is seventeen and David is twelve.

I am a grandfather now. My first grandson was born three months ago.

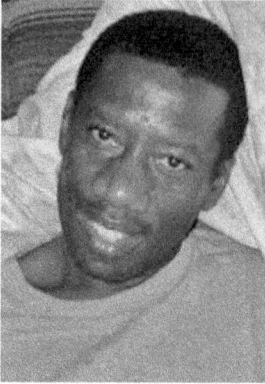

"In the course of my research I discovered that I had no business with the colonial imposition, and I became Jewish."

—Remy Ilona

I am Remy Chukwukaodinaka Ilona, sixth child of Joseph and Paulina Ilona. . . . Chief Azoba, in present-day Anambra State of Nigeria. I was born on third November 1969, a time when the Nigeria-Biafra War was raging.

My mother was more or less a housewife. She didn't have much formal education, but she was a very wise woman. She came from a sort of priestly family. Most of the uncles were doctors and seers. Doctors in native medicine. And some can also "see."[34] It runs in their family. Growing up with that background, my mother understood Igbo society very well.

My father was a civil servant, educated up to middle level. He came from a priestly family, too. It was a kinship system, and we officiated as priests for our extended family. After, when the Igbos started to have kings, they understood ours to be a royal family.[35] Igbos now [take] the Ilonas to be a royal family. My father's father was the undisputed leader of the community.

In 1973—when I was four, five years old—I had a very remarkable experience. My father was talking with a friend about the war that was raging between Israel and the Arab nations.[36] I went to where they were sitting down and said something [that sounded] ignorant to my father. He [yelled], "He's supposed to know everything about it!" He was referring to me. "It is Israel that is at war. My son is supposed to know!" I was just five.

---

[34] That is, they were soothsayers, prophets.

[35] This was a result of the colonial policy of Indirect Rule, which required formal chieftaincies through which the British administrators could then govern the "native" peoples.

[36] The Yom Kippur War.

I observed that talk about Israel was [very] regular in the family. The family must already have had something about Israel, because by the time I came into this world my father was already in his fifties. My elder brother, in Cape Verde now, after greetings the next thing he will start talking about is Israel. (And since Cape Verde is one hundred percent Catholic, he takes his sons to Senegal for circumcision.) You know, the older children of a man would know that man more than the younger children. Since these ones are older than me, it means the family must have had something special about Israel. Israel was unique to them. Basically, Israel is unique to the Igbo people. But more so with my family.

In the early 1970s, after the Biafran war, my father took the family back to Lagos where he was working as staff with the Nigeria Ports Authority. I started school in Lagos [where] I did primary one, two, and three. Then my father moved the family back to Igboland because my father was transferred to Port Hartcourt. But he did not want to move the entire family there. So he moved us to my hometown, where I started school. I stayed in my hometown, which afforded me the opportunity of growing up in a pure Igbo setting, and to witness and observe Igbo customs.

After primary school I progressed to secondary school, still in my hometown, Zobolo. Going to school in my hometown, right in the middle of Igboland, helped me so much prepare for what I am doing presently. Growing up in the Igbo heartland afforded me the opportunity of understanding Elohim and understanding Igbo society.

After I finished secondary school . . . I spent one year at the Institute of Management and Technology in Enugu, studying journalism. [Then] in 1987 I went to my state university—the Anambra State University of Technology—to study law, for four years. In 1991 I went to the law school on Victoria Island in Lagos. After law school, I went into the National Youth Service Corps, from 1992 to 1993.

When I left the Youth Corps, I went into private legal practice in Lagos. After seven years, I moved down to Abuja, to teach law at the outreach centers of the Federal University of Technology at

Owere, and at Ondo State Polytechnic. I taught law at both institutions for one year and decided to study the history of the Igbos,
because while we were growing up we would often hear people
saying one thing or another about "Igbos are the Jews." So I
decided to research that area.

I didn't have much money and decided to deploy all my savings.
My niece here, she came to my aid. My niece made available to
me the sum of one million naira because I had to withdraw from
work. I immediately looked for Jewish groups to assist, but I didn't
know where to begin. All that I was able to lay my hands on is the
statement that the Igbos came from Israel. I did not know how to
begin to research it. You know, I studied law but didn't have proper
research training.

While searching on the Web I ran into one Rivka Adler Lambert.
She was working for the Haifa University office of assistance in
America. I told her what I was about to do. She said that, as a religious Jew, she was fascinated and hoped that what I intended to
do became a reality. It was beneficial, she said, because Israel
needs all the friends it can get. She said she would introduce me to
two Jewish groups, Kulanu organization, and Amishav, now Shavei
Israel. The president of Kulanu then, Jack Zeller, wrote me, saying
he was interested and that I should not relent in my efforts. He introduced me to two Ethiopian Jewish academics, Ethiopian Jews.

Johannes Zeleke is one of the highest ranked archaeologists in
America, one of the key figures in Kulanu. He's a lecturer at American University. The other one is Samuel Tadese. When he was introduced to me, he was with USAID. Both fellows listened to my
story and told me how to go into the subject. They said that if the
Igbos came from Israel, then the evidence would be found in their
religious traditions and in their farming techniques.

I went into research. After six months I released part of it. Dr.
Jack Zeller, the president of Kulanu, wrote back after two days and
said that for six hours he was weeping. What I described was
"quintessentially Israel." I continued my research [with Kulanu
support.]

By then I discovered that a lot of Igbo people had left Christianity and become Jews. I, too—a casual Christian, born into Catholicism but not interested, because my mother was not interested—I, too, discovered Judaism. I [realized] I had no business with the colonial imposition [of Christianity]. I discovered that rabbinical Judaism is the modern version of what my people had practiced. I continued researching and also began acting as *shaliach*[37] for the community. The more I looked, the more I saw. Literally hundreds of synagogues were existing, but they were very small, very small, very small.

It became a passion to share Judaism with as many Nigerians as possible, and I started extending my activities to the universities. Because, what I discovered at the end of the day was that my people's history was subverted. The history of the colonialist was imposed on my people. People were forced to start learning, studying foreign cultures, while our [own] culture was subverted and labeled "pagan." In fact, I think that one may not be able to get close to God if one deviates completely from his own background and culture. Culture has godliness in it.

I also discovered that the best way to revive our culture is to bring it to the universities. Synagogues can go only so far, because the people [at large] have already been indoctrinated into religious fanaticism.

In the course of my foray into Judaism I discovered that Islam was not evil. Growing up Christian, we were told it was evil. Judaism inculcates tolerance in you. . . . To a large extent, Islam is Judaism globalized.[38] Islam has much more in common with Judaism than it does with Christianity. We pray that the problem in the Middle East will be solved. . . .

---

[37] Hebrew for "emissary."

[38] Professor Ali Mazrui (2008) makes a similar point in his maverick *Euro-Jews and Afro-Arabs. The Great Semitic Divergence in World History*. See also his novel (1971) which, in an early postmortem of the Biafran war, includes some "Judaic" references among his wider invocations of Igbo history and culture. For an explanation of Igbo nationalist appropriation of Jewish identity through the prism of suffering, genocide, and renewal (Diaspora, Holocaust, Zionism), see Harnischfeger (2011) and Miles (2004: 382-383).

After three, four, five years of this work I was able to write five books on the subject.

Nri are the primary, priestly class of the Igbos. I would say that they are descended from the tribe of Levi. They are the Levites of the Igbos. Even the name they the Nri people bear in Nigeria is related to a curse that Jacob gave to Levi when he was blessing the twelve sons. God told Levi, "You have [dishonored] Israel. I will scatter you in Israel. You will have no land."[39] The Nri people are scattered all over Igboland, among all Igbos. Their job is to perform priestly functions. The nickname of their town [translates as] "We have no land." Just as the Levites do not have a land in Israel.

In 2002 my niece gave me money and I went to Mwri. I made a friend there, called Obudulou. He assembled all the elders of the community, the real old men, and asked them to tell me about Igbo traditions and Igbo history. The five men or so who spoke, their stories were identical—that the Igbo people came from Israel. They told me about a group of seven Jews that came from Israel.

For one full day they were performing the religious rituals of the Igbos. They came to a particular Igbo ritual called Ifioegbo, and described a special ceremony that [they performed in front of visiting Israelis, with recording equipment]. They requested for the [ceremony] a fowl, a cockerel. One was brought for them. There was an altar before them.

Now, these elders had not entered any school, had not seen any Bible, had not been to Israel. Probably had not seen a Jew in their life. Pure illiterates. The type that Igbos would call "pagans," but the type that we know now to be "Hebrewists." The religion was Judaism but Hebrewism. The Igbo practice of Torah is related more to the type that Moses lay down, not rabbinical Judaism.

When the cockerel was brought, they requested gin and poured libations. Then they requested a sharp knife. When it was brought, they requested it be sharpened, so that the chicken would die with just one cut. They got the chicken, slit the throat, poured the blood

---

[39] See Genesis 49:5–7.

on the altar, and started to remove the feathers and to gum [smear] the blood of the feathers. At that point, the Israelis were transfixed, watching and recording. Then the elders took a feather from near the crop[40] and circled their heads with it, twice. Then they threw the feather aside.

According to the elders, the seven Israelis rose into the air, screaming "*Kaparot, kaparot!*[41] This is Israel! This is Israel!" I requested that the same ritual be performed in my presence. It was performed, I have it on tape. The man who led [the ritual] died the next year, aged ninety-one.

My own decision to enter Judaism was influenced by Ahav Eliyahu, an African-American. While growing up Christian in the United States, he discovered in secondary school that there were a lot of differences between him and the regular Christians. For example, the Christians were not circumcised, but he was. In his late twenties, he began to discover why he was different from the regular Christians. Somebody told him about Jews, and circumcision. So he met Kulanu, and Kulanu introduced us to each other. He introduced me to books of Jewish history, like *The Dead Sea Scrolls*. When I began to read these books, I was able to discover answers—that Jesus was a Jew! If Jesus were to reenter the world, he would not recognize Christianity.

---

[40] "A pouched enlargement of the gullet of many birds, serving as a receptacle for the food and for its preliminary maceration" (*Webster's Collegiate Dictionary*).

[41] *Kaparot* is the ritual observed the day before Yom Kippur (nowadays, rarely so) by which a fowl is waved over the head three times as offering or atonement before slaughtering it.

"In London I told them I was a Jew, that I am practicing Judaism. But they did not allow me into their synagogue. So instead I am gradually converting the Messianics there to the truth, to Torah, to Orthodox Judaism."
—*Shalomith née Kate Chukuma*

My name is Kate Chukuma. My Hebrew name is Shalomith. I was born in Imo State, Nwerre, in 1945. George Obarra was my father, my mother Rachel Obarra. I grew up Anglican. I attended Ebu Primary School. My father died, and so did my mother. So my grandmother raised me.

In 1964 I married Sylvester Chukuma. He was also Anglican, from Anambra State. We had seven children, six boys and one girl.

In 1971, after the Nigerian civil war, I entered one spiritual church. They worshiped both Saturday and Sunday—some on Saturday, some on Sunday. But I read from the Bible that Shabbat day is the real day. So we switched to complete Shabbat worship, as God would have it. Everybody worshiping Shabbat together, on the same day. That's how I began keeping Shabbat.

After that, I began praying to God: "I want to worship You, the true way. The way You want." That was in Enugu, when I was living with my husband. After he died, in 1995, I went to Obusi, a small town. There, I entered Shabbat Church. From there I met one man, Emanuel Mbamago. We were in training together, for that Shabbat mission. We each went away but then came back and started a Messianic church, the two of us. People started following. From there we went to Enugu, where we opened a Shabbat Messianic church.

Someone introduced me to Ephraim Uba. He had a synagogue, Jewish Faith, and I started training in Orthodox [Judaism] with a certain Sambrose. He taught me to wash hands. His wife taught me to make challah.[42] . . .

---

[42] Braided bread baked for and eaten on Shabbat.

I left for London in 2004. My first son was living there so I went to live with him and his wife. . . . When I reached London I told my son I wanted to join Jewish people in worship. He said, "Okay. I know the place where Jewish people worship Shabbat, so you can worship as you like."

He took me to their congregation. I told them I was a Jew, that I am practicing Judaism. But they did not cooperate with us. They did not allow me into their synagogue. They would ask, "Who is your rabbi? Who is your teacher?" They said I must go for conversion. But even after four, five years they do not allow me to come to their synagogue to worship. In Nigeria it is easier to follow my Jewish people.

We joined a Messianic church instead, Mount of Yahweh. Members are mainly African people. The person in charge is Moshe Akwaba, an Igbo. There are many Kenyans, and there is a branch in Kenya. [Back in Nigeria], Ephraim told me to stay there, to use the Messianic church in London for some small time. God would use me to show them Judaism. So I told [the Messianics in London] about the truth, about Torah. They didn't believe me [at first].

But gradually I have converted them to Orthodox. To worship the way of the Creator. We have Shabbat meal. They wear kippa. They wear tallit. They are using *Chumash*. They are going on Internet to seek more.

One year I came back to Nigeria for Pesach festival. I came with matzot and other items for the holiday. I came to Ephraim's synagogue. There I met Rabbi Gorin [visiting from America]. Ephraim connected Igbo Jewish to Gorin. He also connected us to Habakkuk. Rabbi Gorin gave many gifts of books. . . . With the help of Adonai, I am learning Hebrew small small.

> **"There's no point in deceiving the peo-
> ple. The important thing is Shabbat,
> when the Creator Himself rested and
> asked us to do so as well! We were
> told 'it has been changed.' But going
> through the Bible myself, I didn't see
> where it has been changed."**
> *—Yehoshua ben David né Elekwa*

My Hebrew name is Yehoshua ben David. My Igbo name is
Elekwa. I was born in 1959 in Ubweke, Bendel Local Government,
in Abia State. My mother's name is Ori Ayim. My family are
farmers.

I left secondary school in 1978. I did my Higher National
Diploma in Business Admin in 2006. Presently I am in the Federal
Capital Development Authority [FCDA] as an executive officer.
As my brother said, I used to know Lawrence Okah, a friend, from
FCDA. We used to see each other in our offices. He introduced the
tract that talked about the Name [of God], Shabbat, and the Laws.
We would discuss it. [But what we were doing according to the
tract was as a Christian denomination, not keeping Jewish Law.]

Thanks to Lawrence Okah, we had a connection with an American Messianic teacher, Israeli Hawkings, a preacher. He was sending us some of his newspapers, teaching Laws, talking about why
the name of the Christian God—Yehosh[u]a[43]—has nothing to do
with true worship of the Creator. That means what the Christians
are calling God is not really the Name, is not really pleasing the
Creator. We were really not worshiping the Creator. From that
point, I showed my brother the tract. I gave him, he read, and we
started discussing about this issue while going to Church.

I was a leader in the Church at the time, the Deeper Life Bible
Church, headed by W. F. Kumuyi. I was a pastor. One of the
strongest churches in Nigeria.

So most of the other leaders came to me, and I said, "This is

---

[43] Yehoshua (Joshua) is the longer form of the Hebrew name Yeshu (Jesus).

very plain when you look at it. What we are doing is deceiving people. It is not truth. Look at the important thing, Shabbat. That is when the Creator Himself rested and asked us to rest as well! And we were saying 'it has been changed.'" But going through [the Bible], I didn't see where it has been changed. There's no point in deceiving the people.

Then we decided to be meeting together for Fellowship on Shabbat morning. On Shabbat morning we would gather, until evening, until night. Then we went to our brother [Lawrence Okah], who was our first leader. But he was still going to his church. We went to him, to convince him. "You know the truth! You are the one who showed us these things. How do you feel? We cannot stand telling people what we know are lies, and pretend that it is the truth! There's no point." So then he bought our idea, and he stood with us in his place [for worship].

We continued like that, to celebrate the Feasts, the Festivals— Sukkot, Pesach. We would organize, meet. We even went on the air, and told the [listeners] about our new finding. Some of them believed us, and started worshiping with us together.

And so then the time came when [Okah] decided to opt out. We were just managing, because of accommodation. Because [Okah] was no longer with us, and we had no [large enough] place to gather. For a while we were not worshiping together. We would meet on ordinary days, meet to discuss issues in each others' houses, learn Torah.

We began receiving more tracts from various groups in America. We continued to study, to learn new things. . . . And from the traditional [point of view], we realized that we [already] had what you call Pesach. In our own tradition we have what we call in our own language "Eating of Bread." And it is done at the same time as in Israel. And most of our feasts are eight days. We start from what we call éké, and then go until the next éké, eight days.

And again, we have what I believe you call Shavuot—Weeks. After some weeks, we do a Greater One [i.e., gathering, holiday]. In fact, that's when this thing is summarized. After some weeks, there is a presentation of a lot of things. At that time, women would be giving to their husbands, we should be holding meetings, and women prepare new things for husbands. And the New Year. The New Year is the same time. September period. We would do the same thing. When it is getting night, everybody would enter inside. Then we will hear a sound.[44] Then everyone would go out and be joyous, that the New Year has come.

So slowly, as we entered this faith, we found out, "Yes, we have come, this is where Hashem wants us to be." All the ups and downs, all the troubles, frustrations, disappointments—still, all those things do not deter us. We continue, and, as Hashem would have it, we believe we are progressing.

Our brethren from Israel have been helping us. They have really been very helpful. All the knowledge we have, the books we have, they have been giving us for free. They bring us to their synagogue.[45] They are encouraging us. It is a wonderful experience. And our wives truly have been very supportive. . . . Hashem has done so much for us.

With the aid of Hashem, there was a book, *Teach Yourself Hebrew*. Our first leader made a photocopy of that book, and we made [other] photocopies. We started to read, and then to sound the letters, with the vowel points. That's how we continued to improve, day by day. The joy of learning the language, to use it for prayer. Because we believe that it is a heavenly language.

---

[44] Others, in their accounts, will explicitly mention that the sound comes from the blowing of a ram's horn.

[45] Private Israeli construction companies (e.g., SCC, RCC, Gilmor) are quite active in Nigeria.

"Yes, learning Hebrew presents difficulties, but that is very natural. When you are out of the mainstream, it takes time and efforts to realign."

—Zadok ben Yakov
aka Pius Ferguson-Umeh

My Hebrew name is Zadok ben Yakov. My surname—it is a compound name —is Ferguson-dash-Umeh. Pius is my first name. I have Chukodi as my Igbo name. There is another one name, Chukuka. I hail from a town called Umunzee in Orumba South Local Government of Anambra State. Profession—businessman. I was born on October 9, 1963. I came from a dynasty of priests, as it were. My ancestors led the spiritual environment of my place. They stopped at my father, Ferguson-Umeh. He embraced Christianity and was of the Anglican Communion.

When I was growing up, I had a preference for Catholicism. I attended a Catholic primary school. At that point I wasn't very keen attending churches, or church programs. Even in secondary school I stopped attending services and church program.

Sometime in 1982 I had an experience of what they called conversion, or repentance. At first I was in a Pentecostal church, owned by O. Ezekial. But I left it to be among the earlier people who followed Deeper Life Bible Church (and then called Deeper Life Christian Ministry). We pioneered the erection of Deeper Life Bible Church. From Deeper Life I went to one or two other Pentecostal churches. Then I was in Lagos. In 1991 I was in Suleja, Niger State, and joined a New Generation Church. I began to have some discomforts about Christendom. Finally, I lost interest.

Somewhere around in 1993 or 1994, I was associating with Jehovah's Witnesses. I allowed them to come to my house, to my apartment. At one of the occasions of visit, Pinchas, [sitting] here, came in with my neighbor, my next door neighbor, who is presently

part of us in the present faith. I had the discussion with the Jehovah's Witness people, and Pinchas took interest. Maybe he already
had an interest then in the new understanding, that is, the Messianic, which was prominent at that point in time.

After the departure of the Jehovah's Witness people, he discussed with me. From then we started holding meetings on what
we called "Messianic Judaism." The [meetings] were held promi-
nently in my apartment, and we would rotate. Sometimes we would
go to his place, sometimes to [another].

When I was, kind of, infatuated, about the new idea of worship,
I got wind of better places in Lagos. At that point in time I was
free, so I decided to relocate to Lagos so that I would have close
proximity, where I could have access, to places to worship. That
was in the year 2001.

When I got to Lagos, I explored the various places. Messianic
Judaism was practiced. I was not fully convinced and satisfied.
What I have gone to look for was lacking, even though I didn't actually know what I was looking for. So I decided to inquire. I never
entered [a synagogue] until a year and six months ago, when a
friend took me somewhere to Suru-Lere where I first had contact
with Orthodox Judaism.

My friend [Pinchas] in Abuja, with whom I had [remained] in
contact, was telling me that there was already in Abuja a place
where such good experiences could be obtained. At his prompting,
I made haste to come back to Abuja.

So he took me to Gihon. I observed the system of worship there.
I felt convinced that it rose to the level of observance that
[I sought]—at least it measured up to the expectations of my mind.
It was large, and it satisfied my curiosity of the true worship. That
was some months back.

Worshiping in Hebrew, yes—when I got to Gihon, I was enthu-
siastic about being in a place where the true worship is being
observed. That is the primary thing that spurred me. I don't understand Hebrew. But within these few days that happened, with my
own effort, I think I can pronounce, or sound some words, in Hebrew. For now I don't have the materials to read. We just discussed

that today. Perhaps in a few days to come I will have access to those materials that would aid me to understand and read Hebrew. Yes, learning Hebrew presents difficulties, but that is very natural—when you are out of the mainstream, it takes time and efforts to realign. . . . I am fulfilled to a large extent that I am in a right and proper place where I will at least conform with my mindset about the true worship.

CHAPTER FOUR

Tour of a Jubo Shrine

The ritual side of Hezekiah's bar mitzvah would be very familiar to anyone acquainted with normative Judaism—the prayers, the ritual garb, the structure of the service, the reading of the Torah, the use of Hebrew, the melodies. The bar mitzvah reception would be recognizable to anyone acquainted with Nigerian society—the formality and length of the speeches and presentations, the seating arrangements according to seniority and age cohorts, the generous portions of goat meat and rice (I went for the fish), the exuberance of the dancing. What happened afterwards provided a unique window into my host Sar Habakkuk's Igbo-ness and his intensely personal, prophetic approach to Judaism.

Igbo embrace of monotheism was supposed to supplant traditional religious practices that the Western world considered reprobate. The Israeli embassy in Nigeria happens to be located on a street named for Mary Slessor, the Scottish missionary credited with eradicating the custom of putting infant twins to death, practiced in order to combat devilry. Although the origin of "voodoo" is usually associated with the other main ethnic group of southern Nigeria, the Yoruba, Igbo culture, too, has been tainted by it. And in certain circles, it still is. Suspicions linger locally that black magic is still practiced in the recesses of Igbo society. Igbos them-

selves—including Jubos—must therefore be sensitive to any suggestion that it has made even the slightest inroad into Nigerian Judaism. "We don't bring voodoo into the synagogue," one member
of Gihon assured me. "With the Sefer Torah, and the blessing of
Hashem, we keep voodoo out." But why did he bring it up in the
first place? "One member of the congregation was accused of practicing voodoo against another one." He went on to explain:

"In an environment of such poverty, we are told so much about
wizards and witchcraft. There is so much sickness, people live in
fear. They are afraid and want a shortcut, a mystical shortcut.
That's why we need to establish a truly Jewish synagogue."

Given the idiosyncratic nature of the modern path of Igbos to
Judaism, and Habakkuk's keen awareness of the particularities of
his society and faith, he is proactive about diffusing any possible
misunderstandings about his religious faith and practice. His son's
bar mitzvah, and the receiving of guests from far and wide, was
the occasion to do just that. So Habakkuk unhinged the barrier to
the small hut attached to the covered outdoor patio that serves in
season as a sukkah, and he gave selected guests a tour of his
shrine.[1]

"This is my chamber. I want to show my senior friends, so that
they know what I am, and what I am doing. I don't have much in
the way of secrets, as some might think. If someone sees this place
from the outside, they might think that maybe there is some hidden
'something' there. Or maybe that is where I worship my idol. No!
Here is my shrine, where I enter privately and talk to my God. Personally! This is where I go consult my Father.

"I don't allow just anyone to come here, especially those who
don't know anything. There are categories of people. That is why
I said, 'Let the elders see in case they are hearing about Habakkuk,
and that is more hot [i.e., becoming contentious, upsetting]. What
is he doing in there? He is practicing evil.' You will now tell them,
'No. I have witnessed with my eyes.' That is why I have brought

---

[1] I had been privileged to be given a personal tour of the shrine during my
first visit in 2009. Here I combine the commentaries from both.

you people here today." His guests thank him, bless him.

"Shalom. Whatsoever you see, keep it secret with you. Do not discuss it with anybody."

The walls are draped with curtains of blue and white stripes, reminiscent of the tallit, the ritual prayer shawl. Rising a foot or two from the far end on the floor, and wrapping along two adjoining sides, is blue-and-white painted plaster platform. On the top is written, in Hebrew letters, the words for Israel and Nigeria. Leaning on the plaster, on all three sides, are alternating blue and white stones, one for each Hebrew letter, which is painted on each stone in red.[2]

In the center of the shrine, lying on a tiled floor, is a blue, six-sided Star of David, with white center. In the center of the star, in a circle, are twelve blue stones. The plaster Star of David is surrounded by a white-linked chain, at whose base are affixed two crossed swords (blue handles, white blades). In front of the fenced Magen [Hebrew: shield of] David are unpainted stones, shofars (rams' horns, typically blown to usher in the Jewish New Year), and a candle, the type used to herald the Sabbath.

Along the sides of the floor are familiar rituals of Judaica: kiddush cup, Hebrew Bible. There is also a bottle of spirits, a collection of shot glasses, bottles of herbs, and what looks like an upended calabash. But we shall see that it is a hollowed out stone.

Habakkuk circles the inside of the shrine. "I call this place Magen. You can see the twelve tablet stones. They represent Israel.

"Can you read the writing over there? 'Israel in Nigeria'. I am proud to be a Jew. This chain, with Israel [written] in the center, means unity."

He points to a plastic white chair, draped with animal hides. "This is where I chant, where I say my prayers."

The tour continues. "You see this stone?" Habakkuk indicates what I thought was a shell, or a calabash, but is actually a large

---

[2] Habakkuk would later tell me that at first he didn't know why he had collected these stones for his shrine. But after doing so he realized that there were twenty-two of them. (Twenty-two is the number of letters in the Hebrew alphabet.)

rock. "It represents the world. I don't normally remove it, but I will show you." Habakkuk lifts the "big stone" to reveal three smaller ones. "These represent the Law, the statutes, and the ordinances. This is what gives the world problems—if you remove any one of these, if you go against them, it disrupts the world."

He points to other stones, which together make up the tetragrammaton.

"This is the Holy Name of the Almighty Father, Blessed is He . . ."

"Blessed is He," repeat some of the elders.

". . . Yud, hey, vav, hey," he recites, naming the four Hebrew letters that make up the ineffable Name.

There is a seven-stemmed candelabrum. "Whenever I look at it, I remember the Holy Temple."

The candle? "The candle gives light. So whenever I wish to pray at night, I can see."

He points to a shot glass. "This is the cup of Eliyahu [Elijah]. No one drinks from it. But this is my cup," he says, picking up another one. "With it, I bless my ancestors, Abraham, Isaac, and Jacob, and the rest of the saints. The rabbis, who have passed. I bless them, with my drink."

Habakkuk shows his stock of herbs. "I make use of roots and leaves." He pours a liquid into one of the glasses. "It's for health."

He points to the *shofarot*. "Whenever I look at these two rams' horns, I remember the sacrifice of Isaac. You now see where I am going? Whenever I look at them, I remember when Hashem said, 'Touch not that boy!' And Abraham looked around and saw a lamb in the thicket. This is what made Abraham to be a trustworthy man. He was ready to slaughter his boy, just to fulfill the word of the Almighty Father.

"Whenever you look at it, it means a lot. When I started meditating over this, my spirit is telling me, 'This is why Yisrael must be saved.' At the time of judgment, Hashem will say, 'Blow the horn!' Hashem will free all Israel. Because of Isaac."

Habakkuk completes the circle of the shrine. "This sword represents war, misunderstanding, in the midst of Israel. This is our

Inside Habakkuk's shrine

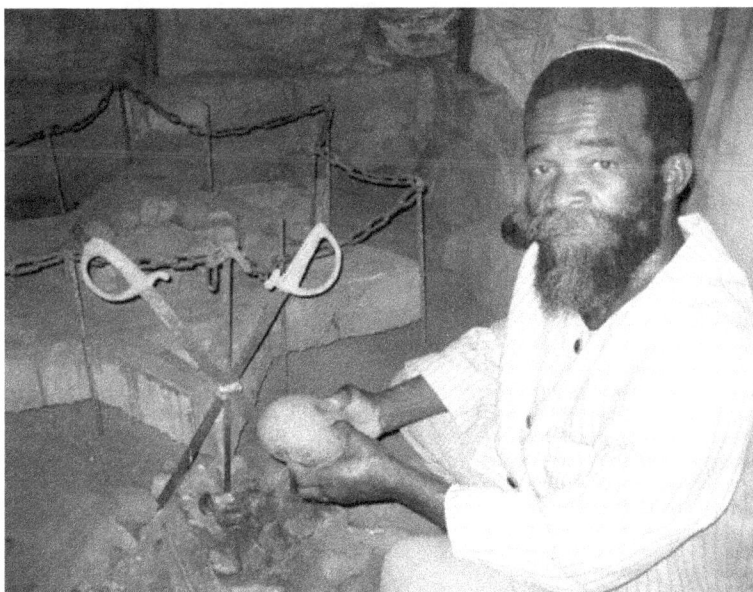

Habakkuk in shrine

prayer today, for Hashem to remove this sword, so that peace will prevail over the land of Israel. Because Israel is not in peace now. May Hashem give Israel peace.

"Whenever I enter here," Habakkuk concludes, "I am full of spirit. Even if someone is dying.

"You have witnessed it now." Habakkuk reminds the elders of the reason why he opened up the shrine to them: "You know what I am doing. In case people say, 'Habakkuk [does] this, Habakkuk [does that].' You know it now. My power comes from Hashem, not from anywhere else. So Israel, Peace Be Unto You."

Before exiting Habakkuk's shrine—an unusual spot amongst an unusual people—one of the Jubo elders gives his blessing. "The whole thing is in order. It is self-explanatory. It is personally meant for you and for the Almighty. It is for the truth, and for all those who understand the truth." The guests exit the shrine, seemingly satisfied.

I observe to Habakkuk, "You have made some changes since the last time I visited." He has added several items to the shrine, but he focuses particularly on the representations of angels: "So that they will be helping me, in answering some of my prayers. They are the angels of creation. They are my friends.

"Why not make changes?" he adds, upon reflection. "We don't need to remain [the way we are]. We grow every day."

* * *

On the day following the tour of his shrine, Habakkuk reveals yet another side of his identification with Torah. For Jews more used to sidling up to a reading from the Five Books of Moses, or following along as a Haftorah[3] portion is chanted at Saturday morning services, his personal way of engaging Torah might be a bit unsettling. As Habakkuk recounts the extraordinary trajectory of his life, we realize we are in the presence of one who unabashedly lives

---

[3] A chapter from Prophets, the second section of the Old Testament, read after the Torah.

out a contemporary version of *Tanach* (Old Testament). Here is a Jew who believes—as did Abraham, the progenitor of the Jewish religion and people—that God speaks to us, and calls us for a purpose. Here is a Jew who does not consign prophets and prophesying to the Jewish past. But the way to Hashem is not always direct.

"God is by my side. . . . Before, I was a businessman. I traded, did well, but then fell down. I entered the transport business, did well at first but again failed, on account of the wickedness of others. They caused an accident, a bonfire, and engine failure.

"Despite my age, I started all over again as a driver, then in a construction company. I have children so I couldn't retire. It is then that my first daughter fell sick. She was about two.

"I took her to hospital, but they could not find a cure. And so, one Saturday, I went to a prayer house near there—Messianic Shabbat Keepers.

"The prophetess woman at that prayer house told me that the Holy One of Israel wanted me. That is why He did not have the doctor cure my girl. So that I would find Him. So that I would come where they worship Him, on a Shabbat day. She also told me that I was going to become a special servant of God. I couldn't accept the word of one witness alone, but starting that day I became a Shabbat Keeper—as a Messianic. For a long time I put my head and everything I had into Shabbat keeping. I am a hard-working man.

"Four years later another prophet came into my life. It was the man who later would teach me *aleph-bet*—'Rabbi'[4] Moshe ben Luwyi. He came to Nigeria to give a seminar. In that place there are *so many* prophets! During the meeting he pointed to me in the back. 'Who is this man there? Call him!' Everyone was looking at me. Even I myself was looking behind, to see who he was calling. But people were touching me. 'Yes,' he said. 'You come!' I came forth.

---

[4] Appropriation by Messianics of the honorific "rabbi" has been one of the sources of confusion about Judaism in Nigeria.

"'Do you know this man?' he asked. People responded. 'Yes, we know him. We know him as Habakkuk.'

"'No,' he said. 'This man is not Habakkuk. This man is Sar Habakkuk ben Melchizedek. This man is called as a priest to represent Melchizedek.'[5] That day he anointed me. As a Messianic. I was told to start praying, and that when I did so for a sick person, that person would be healed.

"After that I came down here to Abuja. A small time later, one of my friends, Keesh, came to me with a problem. I prayed for him, and God answered the prayer. He then told me: 'For the sake of God—Who answers your prayer—you have a call.' Keesh is the person who introduced Judaism to me. 'This is the right way,' he said. Not 'Messianic' Judaism, but actual Judaism.

"I have a flexible spirit, and I have a flexible mind. When I see the truth, I follow it immediately. I looked at the Jewish religion and then joined. . . .

"The business I do now is Hashem's business. When I pray, Hashem answers. 'Do this,' I do. When I pray, whatever the spirit tells me to do, I do. And when I do, knowledge increases in the spirit. It's like magic."

Examples?

"There was this brother. He belonged to a dangerous society. One day his brain was off. He pulled off his cloth and ran through the street.

"People caught him and brought him here to me. After only two weeks his brain came back. He was a mad man and I made him free. (After that he attacked me spiritually but he failed.)" Habakkuk then goes on to speak of a woman who had come to his homestead the day before.

"That mother who you saw yesterday? She was also attacked spiritually. Her leg became defective. But I healed her.

"I go into the bush," Habakkuk adds, explaining the contents of

---

[5] In the book of Genesis, Melchizedek is a priest-king who blessed Abraham after his return from battle and offered him bread and wine. Christianity holds Melchizedek as the model of clerical rulership in the new order.

the bottles and bags I observed with great interest in the shrine. "I find roots, leaves. I give them to the sick, and they get better. That's how I earn my money, through prayer.

"At times I travel to the east to pray. I ask Hashem for what I want so that I can use my talent and experience to help Jews." On account of economic conditions and the relatively small size of the community, however, Habakkuk cannot limit his practice to assisting only other Jews. "If you relied only on the Jews, you would die of hunger." But he doesn't accept payment from Jubos, only from his non-Jewish clients.

* * *

This is the testimony of Sar Habakkuk's life and family:

"Hashem loves me. He gave me my beautiful wife who hearkens to the instruction of Hashem, and also hearkens to my own instruction. She obeys Hashem and obeys me at the same time.[6] I believe anybody who has the chance to have a Jewish wife Hashem has blessed. The worst mistake one can make in life is to marry a woman who does not suit one.

"Some time ago, when my son Hezekiah was no older than five, a friend stopped by on a Friday. This man would always come on Shabbat, and we would worship together. His wife was not yet Jewish.

"He came, we discussed, and we took food as one family. He was about to arrange himself to leave, to prepare for the Shabbat morrow, when I came out from my shrine. An angel came over and whispered to me: 'This man is condemned. He is going to die today.'

"What?!

"'Nothing will stop it,' the angel replied. Kai!

"So I went back into the shrine to discuss. I said, 'Father, is this true?'

---

[6] As his own testimony bears out, Habakkuk in fact consults with and seeks counsel from his wife.

"'It is destined.'

"'Is it [upon leaving] the synagogue that he will die?'" Was Habakkuk trying to shame God? At any rate, like Abraham, like Jeremiah, like so many exemplars of the stiff-necked people, Habakkuk argued with Him.

"'What do You think people will say? What would the wife think? What happens to this man is what his wife and family will say of You. This is not proper. It would be blasphemous. It would be Your Name blasphemed!'

"The Holy One of Israel, blessed is He, hearkened to me. Just as my friend was about to return home on his machine,[7] the angel called me and said, 'The only remedy against this man dying is that he be accompanied by a virgin boy. That Hashem consider him pure, like a virgin boy.'

"That is when I confirmed, really, that this woman, my wife, was destined for me. I called her over and told her, 'The signboard of death is placed on our guest's back. But I've been praying. And the only answer is what the angel told me.'" After explaining the condition to his wife, he turned to her for consent. "'Let me give him Hezekiah, to follow him home, so that he not die.'"

Habakkuk's wife did not balk. "'If it is the wish of God,' she decided, 'so be it.'"

Habakkuk called for his son. "'Hezekiah! Escort this man!'" The little boy climbed onto the "machine" and clung to the back of the visitor. But before they reached the bridge, as Habakkuk vividly recalls, "Accident! The machine is condemned!

"Hezekiah, my son. . . . People went into the gutter to pick him up. There was no more cloth on his body. His trousers and shirt were in the gutter. But none of his body was wounded.

"The man was in the hospital for three days. After Shabbat, on Sunday, I went to see him. He didn't know.[8] He was like a dead man. Same on Monday. Only on Tuesday did he begin to recover and talk. I came home and thanked the Holy One of Israel. My

---

[7] Nigerian English for a motor scooter or motorcycle.
[8] That is, he was unconscious.

friend stayed in the hospital for one month." Hezekiah was spared. But the real hero, according to Habakkuk, was Hezekiah's mother.

"Who is the woman who will agree to give her only son to save someone's life? Even Abraham didn't tell his wife, Sarah, what he was going to do with Isaac.[9] But I told my wife.

"If my son had died in the accident, this house could not contain me and my wife. In our tradition, a home without a son has no name. . . . I am happy that Hashem did as He did, so that His Name would not be blasphemed."

* * *

Sar Habakkuk is not an ordinary man. He is extraordinary as an Igbo, as a Jubo, as a Jew *tout court*. This is the same Habakkuk who has meticulously arranged for his son to become a bar mitzvah according to the familiar norms and customs of modern Judaism, from reading the Sefer Torah in Hebrew to hosting a big bash party with blue-and-white frosted cake. So seamless is his weaving of the halachic with the prophetic that I nearly overlook it when he casually mentions that his occupation is "spiritual healer."

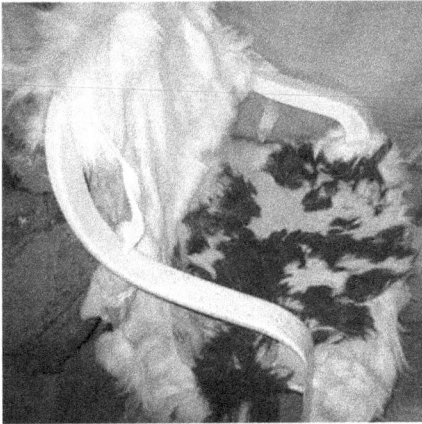

Habakkuk's shrine throne

Habakkuk, as atypical as he is as an individual, personifies Judaism's inordinate capacity to fuse an ancient mindset with complexly evolved rituals and theology. As does Judaism itself, Habakkuk's worldview and practices transcend time, space, and culture. You cannot separate the shema from the shrine.

---

[9] That is, sacrifice him as commanded by God.

Postscript

"Astonishing":
A Conversation with Chinua Achebe

Fewer than three months after Hezekiah's bar mitzvah, I had the opportunity to share my Jubo encounters with the most prominent Igbo in the world of letters: Chinua Achebe. What, I wanted to learn, did Achebe know about his judaizing co-ethnics? What did he make of them?

In his Brown University office on Angel Street in Providence, Rhode Island, Achebe listened, interested but reserved, as I related my findings and experiences amongst his co-ethnics in Abuja. I told him about my first sojourns in West Africa, my Hanukka trip to Abuja, and my return there for Hezekiah's coming-of-age ceremony. He knew in general terms what "bar mitzvah" meant, about rabbis, even about Torah scrolls. He did not, however, know about the Jubos, pronounced the phenomenon "astonishing," and expressed polite desire to learn more about it. It was only after I asked him to show me on my map of Nigeria the town—if he had ever heard of it—from which the fourteen guests and officiants had driven eight hours in a minibus to Abuja with their Sefer Torah that the mood in the room changed from collegial to electric. We stared at each other in silence, now in mutual astonishment, for many long seconds.

"In other times, we would speak of 'mysteries,'" the sage finally commented on the coincidence. For Ogidi, it turns out, is the place that Chinua Achebe calls home, his birthplace, the spot in Igboland where he maintains a residence.

He was unaware, though, of the Igbo Jewish Community Synagogue of Ogidi.

Chinua called into the office his son Ike (pronounced Ee-keh), a doctoral candidate in the United Kingdom, who was visiting. He had been in Ogidi just a few days prior. Ike didn't know about the Jubos of his hometown, either. But my visit reminded both father and son of an almost legendary figure in both Igbo colonial history and Achebe family lore: the Reverend George T. Basden.

Basden spent thirty-five years in Igboland as a missionary. The subtitles of his two books (1921,1938) well reflect the colonial context and proselytizing mindset of that experience, which he related as amateur anthropologist. As our conversation proceeded, Chinua Achebe began to recall the association that Basden used to make between Igbos and Israelites. Even more vividly did he invoke the significance of this English minister for the Achebe community and family: it was Reverend Basden who performed the first Christian wedding in Ogidi—that of Achebe's parents.

Basden's own theory on the link between Igbos and Hebrews is less than categorical:

> I offer the suggestion . . . that the Ibo people . . . at some remote time either actually lived near, or had very close association with, the Semitic Races. The successive waves of invasion from the North-East of Asia down through Egypt pressed these people to the South-West [of Nigeria]. As wave after wave came, they were borne onwards until, finally, the Ibos came to rest where we find them to-day and, throughout the ages, they have retained ideas and customs handed down from generation to generation. (Basden 1938: 414)

Basden (who shows his familiarity with Joseph Williams's [1930] tantalizing but tenuous *Hebrewisms of West Africa*) identifies several parallels between Igbo custom and "Levitical Law": land tenure; the *lex talionis* (an eye for an eye, a tooth for a tooth); rules governing female dress; the Law of Sanctuary; capital punishment (for murder, adultery); postpartum seclusion; menstrual separation; anti-wizardry; sacrifices; rites of atonement; redemption of the firstborn son; and so on. But to the end, he remains prudent in drawing historical, genealogical, conclusions:

> I anticipate that others, and especially my Ibo friends, will discover yet more comparisons and resemblances between Israelitish Law and ancient Ibo custom. It may not be of much significance, and prove no more than coincidence, but it is, nevertheless, an interesting subject. (Basden 1938: 422)

Chinua Achebe seems to share Basden's combination of fascination and skepticism. "The Igbos," the elder Achebe commented, "have great curiosity. When you were telling me about these ones"—the Jews from Ogidi and elsewhere in Igboland—"a smile almost came to my face." A smile of bemusement? He did not specify more. But even Chinua Achebe agreed that the revelation of Igbos practicing Judaism is "something we must look into further."

Bibliography

Achebe, Chinua. 1958. *Things Fall Apart*. New York: Alfred A. Knopf.

Alaezi, O. 1999. *Ibos. Hebrew Exiles from Israel. Amazing Facts and Revelations*. Aba: Onzy Publications.

Basden, G. T. 1921. *Among the Ibos of Nigeria. An account of the Curious & Interesting Habits, Customs & Beliefs of a little known African People by one who has for many years lived amongst them on close & intimate terms*. London: Frank Cass.

_____. 1938. *Niger Ibos. A Description of the Primitive Life, Customs and Animistic Beliefs, &., of the Ibo People of Nigeria By One Who, For Thirty-Five Years, Enjoyed the Privilege of Their Intimate Confidence and Friendship*. London: Frank Cass.

Ben-Jochannan, Yosef et al. 1988. *The Afrikan Origins of the Major World Religions*. London: Karnak House.

Bruder, Edith. 2008. *The Black Jews of Africa. History, Religion, Identity*. Oxford: Oxford University Press.

Buber, Martin. 1970 [1923]. *I and Thou*. Scribner: New York.

Caliben, I. O. Michael. 2011. *Our Roots. Igbo Israel Heritage*. Abuja: OBGI Israel Heritage Foundation.

Dorès, Maurice. 1992. *La Beauté Cham. Mondes juifs, mondes noirs* [The Beauty of Ham. Jewish worlds, Black worlds]. Paris: Editions Balland.

_____. 2003. Black-Israël (documentary film). Paris: Les Films Esdés (producer) and New York: Filmmakers Library (distributor).

_____. 2008. "Identités juives et racines africaines" [Jewish identities and African roots]. In Shmuel Trigano, ed., *Juifs et Noirs. Du mythe à la réalité* [Jews and Blacks: From myth to reality]. *Pardès* 44.

Equiano, Olaudah. 1789/1995. *The Interesting Narrative of the Life of Olaudah Equiano. Written by Himself.* Edited by Robert J. Allison. New York: St. Martin's Press.

Feinberg, Harvey M., and Joseph B. Solodow. 2002. "Out of Africa." *Journal of African History* 43(2): 255-261.

Goldstein, David B. 2008. *Jacob's Legacy. A Genetic View of Jewish History.* New Haven, CT: Yale University Press.

Harnischfeger, Johannes. 2011. "Igbo Nationalism and Biafra." *Afrikanistik online,* Vol. 2011. (urn:nbn:de:0009-10-30425)

Horton, James Africanus. 1868/1969. *West African Countries and Peoples.* Edinburgh: Edinburgh University Press.

Hull, Richard. 2009. *Jews and Judaism in African History.* Princeton, NJ: Markus Wiener Publishers.

Ilona, Remy. 2007. *The Igbos: Jews in Africa. With Reflections on the Civil War and Solutions to the Most Critical Igbo Problem.* Abuja: Counselor International Limited.

_____. 2012. *The Igbos and Israel: An Inter-cultural Study of the Oldest and Largest Jewish Diaspora.* Washington, D.C.: Kulanu, Inc and EpicCenter Stories.

_____. n.d. *Introduction to the Chronicles of Igbo-Israel.* Abuja: Israel-Igbo Publishing Ltd.

Kirsch, Stuart. 1997. "Lost Tribes: Indigenous People and the Social Imaginary." *Anthropological Quarterly* 70(2): 58-67.

Lieberman, Jeffrey. 2012. *Re-Emerging: The Jews of Nigeria.* New York: Re-Emerging Films (producer and distributor).

Lis, Daniel. 2006. "Swiss-Israeli Anthropologist Journeys to Nigeria." www.kulanu.org/nigeria/anthropologist.php

_____. 2009. "'Ethiopia shall soon stretch out her hands': Ethiopian Jewry and Igbo Identity." *Jewish Culture and History* 11(3): 21-38.

Mazrui, Ali A. 1971. *The Trial of Christopher Okigbo.* London: Heinemann.

_____. 2008. *Euro-Jews and Afro-Arabs. The Great Semitic Divergence in World History.* Lanham, MD: University Press of America.

Miles, William F. S. 1993. "Hausa Dreams." *Anthropologica* 35: 105-116.

_____. 1997. "Negritude and Judaism." *The Western Journal of Black Studies* 27(2): 99-105.

_____. 2002. *Third World Views of the Holocaust. Summary of the International Symposium.* Boston: Northeastern University (on-line version:www.violence.neu.edu/projects_and_events/past_conferences/third_world_views).

_____. 2004. "Third World Views of the Holocaust." *Journal of Genocide Research* 6(3): 371- 393.

_____, ed. 2007a. *Political Islam in West Africa. State-Society Relations Transformed.* Boulder, CO: Lynne Rienner Publishers.

_____. 2007b. *Zion in the Desert. American Jews in Israel's Reform Kibbutzim.* Albany: State University of New York Press.

_____. 2008. *My African Horse Problem.* Amherst: University of Massachusetts Press.

_____. 2011. "Among the 'Jubos' During the Festival of Lights." *Transition: An International Review* 105: 30-45.

Miller, Madeleine S., and J. Lane Miller. 1952. *Harper's Bible Dictionary.* New York: Harper & Brothers.

Milligan, Maren. 2008. "Nigerian Echoes of the Israeli-Palestinian Conflict." *ISIM Review* [International Institute for the Study of Islam in the Modern World] 21 (Spring).

Oduyoye, Modupe. 1995. *The Alphabetical Psalms. Systematic Instruction for a Life of Faith and Trust.* Ibadan: Sefer Books.

_____. 1998. *The Sons of the Gods and the Daughters of Men. An Afro-Asiatic Interpretation of Genesis 1-11.* Ibadan: Sefer Books.

Ogbukagu, Ik N. T. 2001. *The Igbo and the Riddles of Their Jewish Origins.* Enugu: Chobikate Nigeria Company.

Palmer, Joanne. 2006. "Becoming Jewish: How a Nice Jewish Boy Became a Chief Rabbi in Nigeria." *United Synagogue Review* Spring/Summer, pp. 27-28.

Perelman, Marc. 2008. "The Ibos of Nigeria: Members of the Tribe?" *The Forward,* October 10.

Pirkei Avoth (*Sayings of the Fathers*). 1945. New York: Behrman House.

Primack, Karen, ed. 1998. *Jews in Places You Never Thought Of.* Hoboken, NJ: KTAV Publishing House in Association with KULANU.

Rosten, Leo. 1968 [and 2001, as *The New Joys of Yiddish*]. *The Joys of Yiddish*. New York: McGraw-Hill.

Rubin, Barry. 1995. *Assimilation and Its Discontents*. New York: Random House.

Telushkin, Joseph. 1992. *Jewish Humor. What the Best Jewish Jokes Say about the Jews*. New York: William Morrow and Company.

Ujah, Charles. 2006. *The Origin of Ibos. From Linguistic and Cultural Angle*. Lagos: Ezbon Communications Ltd.

Umeokolo, Uche Onwumelu. n.d. *Biography of Remy Ilona. The Man Who Worked for Igbo-Israel*. Abuja: Igbo-Israel Publishing Ltd.

Uwaezuoke, Okechukwu. 2011. "Close-up on Nigerian Jews." *This Day* February 13, p. 82.

Wachman, Doreen. n.d. "The Jews of Cameroon." Online two-part article originating with the Jewish Telegraph Group of Newspapers—UK (www.jewishtelegraph.com).

Williams, Joseph. 1930. *Hebrewisms of West Africa. From Nile to Niger with the Jews*. London: Allen and Unwin.

About the Author

William F. S. Miles is professor of political science at Northeastern University in Boston and the former Stotsky Professor of Jewish Historical and Cultural Studies there. *Jews of Nigeria* is his tenth book. A five-time Fulbright scholar, Miles is the author of many Africanist works, including *Hausaland Divided*, *Elections in Nigeria*, and, as editor and major contributor, *Political Islam in West Africa*. Winner of the National Bible Contest and North American representative to the International Bible Contest, William Miles has most recently published *Zion in the Desert* (an ethno-autobiography of the kibbutz movement of Reform Judaism in Israel) and *My African Horse Problem* (a memoir of his and his ten-year-old son's efforts to settle an inheritance dispute in a Muslim village in the Niger-Nigeria borderlands). Husband of Loïza and father of Arielle and Samuel Miles, he lives near the border with Rhode Island (as a member of Temple Emanu-El) in Seekonk, Massachusetts.

Related Books by Markus Wiener Publishers

Jews and Judaism in African History
BY RICHARD HULL
ISBN 978-1-55876-496-5

> "Hull admirably achieves his goal of painting Jews and Judaism
> smoothly into the larger canvas of the continent's history . . ."
> —*African Studies Review*

Jews of a Saharan Oasis:
Elimination of the Tamantit Community
BY JOHN HUNWICK
ISBN 978-1-55876-346-3

> Hunwick examines the debates among Muslim scholars of the region
> over the rights of Jews living among Muslims and provides translations
> of the scholars' Arabic writings.

Africa: A Short History
BY ROBERT O. COLLINS
ISBN 978-1-55876-373-9

> "An elegantly written narrative that takes us from prehistoric times
> to contemporary Africa." —*African Studies Review*

Documents from the African Past
EDITED BY ROBERT O. COLLINS
ISBN 978-1-55876-289-3

> The primary sources in this fascinating collection describe, among
> other historical undercurrents, ancient and medieval trade routes,
> China's discovery of Africa, the slave trade, and the experiences
> of Asian and European settlers, merchants, and colonialists.

Once Jews: Stories of Caribbean Sephardim
BY JOSETTE CAPRILES GOLDISH
ISBN 978-1-55876-494-1

> " . . . a goldmine of historical documents . . . , [this book] is evidence
> that some of the richest historical and sociological sources of the Jewish
> Caribbean are in the hands and mouths of its Sephardic descendants."
> —*New West Indian Guide*

www.ingramcontent.com/pod-product-compliance
Lightning Source LLC
Chambersburg PA
CBHW031445280326
41927CB00037B/303